J.J. McCarthy

The Story of Exploration and Adventure in Africa

J.J. McCarthy

The Story of Exploration and Adventure in Africa

ISBN/EAN: 9783744758208

Printed in Europe, USA, Canada, Australia, Japan

Cover: Foto ©Andreas Hilbeck / pixelio.de

More available books at **www.hansebooks.com**

KAFFIR MAN AND WOMAN.

Half a century ago the sources of the Nile were unexplored, the great lake system of Equatorial and Southeastern Africa was unknown, the Mountains of the Moon, which find a place in Ptolemy's map as the source of the Nile, were regarded as mythical, though Stanley's discoveries would seem to have identified them with Mount Gordon Bennett (discovered in 1876), and Ruwenzori (the Snowy Mountain, near or on the Equator), which he discovered on his last journey. Then the Niger and Congo have been traced through a great portion of their courses, and Livingstone taught us most of what we know of the chief river of Southern Africa, the Zambesi.

The first geographical system of Africa which deserves the name, is that of Herodotus, the "Father of History," who gave a full description of these regions, and the accuracy of his reports have received singular confirmation by more recent discoveries. The Nile figured as the great feature in the system of Herodotus, and he described, with tolerable correctness, the northwest of Africa as far as the Straits.

Herodotus tells us that the Egyptian King, Necho, sent out an expedition with the design of circumnavigating Africa. Nothing is known as to whether or not they accomplished their purpose. The Phœnicians are known to have formed colonies on the northern coast more than 3000 years ago.

The next geographical system was that of Ptolemy, who flourished in the second century. To Ptolemy is due the theory that the Nile has its sources in the Mountains of the Moon, under or beyond the Equator, and he depicts in his map the lakes through which the river flows, thus in a remarkable manner shadowing orth the discoveries of Speke, and Baker, and Stanley. He also represents the junction of the Blue Nile of Abyssinia with the White Nile at Meroe, which he makes into an island. Westward he describes the vast Libyan desert as watered by the Gir and Niger, spoken of as " rivers of the greatest magnitude," the former of which might have been the Gambia or Senegal River.

Ptolemy, therefore, is entitled to the credit of being the first of the ancients to show that the Nile and Niger were distinct rivers, one having its sources far to the southward, and the Niger, he says, forms the lake of Nigritia, which lies in latitude 15°, longitude 18°, thus clearly denoting its source from Lake Tchad.

Respecting Northern Africa, our first authentic information comes from the Arabs, who, by means of the camel (the ship of the desert), crossed the great desert to the centre of the continent, and proceeded along the two coasts as far as the Senegal and the Gambia on the west, and to Sofala on the east. The Arabs planted colonies here and elsewhere.

In the fifteenth century there was a new era in maritime discovery. The Portuguese were the first to give an accurate outline of the two coasts, and to complete the circumnavigation of the continent. The discovery of America and the West India Islands gave rise to the traffic in African negroes. Nefarious as is this traffic, it was the means of obtaining an accurate knowledge of the coast as it lies between the Rivers Senegal and the Cameroons. Systematic surveys of the coast and the interior followed the French and English settlements in Africa.

A few learned and scientific gentlemen in England

African Association," their design being the exploration of Inner Africa. Owing to the efforts of this Association, important additions were made to the geography of Africa, by Houghton, Mungo Park, Hornemana, and Burckhardt. Repeated failures discouraged the society, and it was merged into the Royal Geographical Society in 1831. Much more has been done in the last 65 years to make us acquainted with Africa than was accomplished in the preceding 18 centuries. With Mungo Park begins the era of increasing endeavors to explore the interior. A resume of the travels from Park down to the present time will be detailed in the present volume.

In 1892 the area of Africa was given as 11,600,000 square miles; and its population was estimated at 192,520,000.

Africa is a land of deserts. The Nile is the oldest of historical rivers, and afforded the only means of subsistence to the earliest civilized people on earth, and yet the origin of this river remained an enigma almost to the present day. It is one of the largest rivers of the globe, having a course of about 4000 miles, and draining over a million of miles in Africa. The other great rivers are the Congo, the Niger, and the Zambesi.

Lake Tchad is the largest of the lakes. It is situated nearly in the centre of the continent: it is about 220 miles long, and at its widest point is 140 miles broad. At some seasons it is nearly dry.

The climate of Africa, particularly in the rainy zone, is entirely uniform, and by reason of its position (four-fifths in the tropics), of the large extent of Sahara within the hot zone, and of the small water-supply and the limited area of the forests, it is extremely dry and hot.

TRAVELERS AND THE MIRAGE.

The interior of Africa is in all probability the hottest region on the globe, but exhibits great contrasts of temperature. The days often reach a temperature of 125° Fahrenheit, yet the nights sometimes have only 55°. In the extreme northern and southern parts, the four seasons of the temperate zone are found. The supply of rain is very scanty. The deserts of Sahara and Kalahari are almost rainless.

The animal life is distinguished by large and clumsy forms. Here are found the elephant and rhinoceros and the hippopotamus. The average weight of a full grown hippopotamus is about 3500 pounds. They abound in all the large rivers. The African lion is the noblest animal of the race. Leopards are numerous and very fierce. Hyenas, ichneumons, and civets are met with. Antelopes are found everywhere, sometimes in herds of 100,000. The camel, the Barbary horse, and the ass are the beasts of burden mostly used. Numerous genera of apes and monkeys are found. The zebra, quagga, and the giraffe, the tallest existing mammal in Central and Southern Africa, are peculiar to the continent. Among birds, the ostrich, described as the feathered camel, or the giraffe among birds, is the most remarkable. Parrots and bright-colored, noisy birds enliven the forests. Among reptiles, the crocodile is found in all the large rivers and lakes. Various species of serpents and lizards are met with; but they are fewer than in other tropical countries, owing to the dryness of the climate. Among insects, the termites, or white ants, with their cone-like habitations, are most destructive. They attack and demolish everything, but metals and stones, that comes in their way. Locusts are still more destructive. An army of them passing over a country

TERMITES: AN ANT HILL.

leaves it as bare as if it had been swept with a broom. They are used as food by many of the native tribes. Fish in great variety are to be found in most of the rivers and on the coast. On the coast sharks are numerous; as are also black and spermaceti whales.

Mohammedanism and Fetichism are the prevailing religions of Africa, except in Abyssinia, where a corrupt form of Christianity exists. Human sacrifices are offered in some of the negro nations, but rarely except on great occasions. The Mohammedans number from 60 to 100 millions. Jews are numerous in Morocco, Algeria, and Abyssinia; their aggregate in all Africa being about 800,000. The Roman Catholics claim from one to four millions of the population.

Never has the future of Africa been brighter than at the present time. There is no hope for a return of those glories which ages upon ages past adorned Egypt; the might of Carthage has long since gone for ever—the whole of North Africa has been divided, and the signs of improvement are very limited. In other parts of the continent, however, new life is springing, channels for the introduction of civilization are constantly appearing.

The scramble for Africa goes on apace. Italy has secured a firm foothold upon the eastern borders of Abyssinia and has schemes of further conquest by war or negotiation; the influence of France is being felt throughout Algeria. The first months of the year 1891 found the French pushing trade routes beyond Ghadmes and on through the oases of the Sahara Desert to the broad central Soudan; in Senegambia and the West Coast countries, commerce flourishes; the Congo basin teems with trading vessels, as the river will surely do in the near future; almost the whole of South Africa has fallen under British protection. Mashonoland, a vast tract of country owned by the Matabele, north of the Kuruman River, and not very far from the western bends of the Zambesi, has since 1891 come under the sway of the English through the enterprise of the British South Africa Company; in Nyassaland the claims of England are firmly established. In Central Africa, indeed, an expanse—six hundred thousand square miles—of rich territory came within recognized British control in 1890. Germany then received a large slice of country as her share of the bargain.

All this cannot fail to exert a powerful influence for good upon Africa. With still greater strides will Christianity and civilization advance, until the whole continent shall be flooded with their light.

CHAPTER II.

Bruce's Travels in Abyssinia.

To discover the country of Prester John, the mysterious Christian monarch of the East—first supposed to be in Tartary, and then in Abyssinia—and to effect the passage to India, were the chief motives of the voyage in 1486, of Bartholomew Diaz, the first navigator to round the Cape of Good Hope (which he very correctly named Cape Stormy), and of Vasco de Gama, who, twelve years after, voyaged up the east coast of Africa, and passing Mozambique, Mombassa, and Melinda, crossed the Indian Ocean in 23 days, and cast anchor in Calicut, on the Malabar coast.

The first European to penetrate into Abyssinia, of whom we have any record, was the Portuguese Covilham, who was sent on a mission by land to Prester John from the King of Portugal, with the object of inquiring whether it was possible to sail to India from the Cape of Good Hope, which Diaz had recently discovered. Covilham quitted Lisbon in May, 1487, and first visiting India, proceeded to Abyssinia, where he was detained by the King, and held high office in the state. In the year 1525, when Rodriguez de Lima went as Portuguese ambassador to Abyssinia, Covilham was still alive.

JAMES BRUCE.

Lima's secretary, Alvarez, wrote a narrative of his six years' residence in the country, which is of great interest. In this work Alvarez speaks of the King of Abyssinia as Prete Janni, or Prester John.

The Portuguese attained much influence in the country through Payz and other priests of the Roman Catholic Church. Payz has the distinction of discovering the sources of the Blue Nile, known as the Bahr-el-Azrek, to distinguish it from the Bahr-el-Abiad, which D'Anville was the first to point out was the true, or "White Nile." The following passage from Payz's Journal, is of interest, as giving the first description of the so-called fountains of the Nile, which Bruce visited at a later period:—

"The source of the Nile is situated on the elevated point of a valley, which resembles a large plain, surrounded on every side with ridges of hills. While I resided in this kingdom, I ascended this place on April 21, 1618, and took a diligent survey of every part of it. I saw two round fountains, but about five palms in diameter. Great was my pleasure in beholding what Cyrus, King of the Persians, Cambyses, Alexander the Great, and the renowned Julius Cæsar sought eagerly, but in vain, to find. The water is very clear, light and agreeable to the taste; yet these two fountains have no outlet in the higher part of the mountain plain, but only at the foot. The inhabitants say the whole mountain is full of water, which they prove by this: that all the plain about the fountain is tremulous and bubbling—a sure proof of water underneath; and that, for the same cause, the water does not run over the sources, but throws itself out with greater force lower down. The inhabitants affirmed, that, though the ground had trembled little this year on account of the great dryness, yet that in common seasons it shook and bubbled to such a degree as scarcely to be approached without danger.

Payz relates the course of the Nile, the tributaries which it receives, its crossing lake Dembea, with a visible separation of waters, the tremendous cataract of Alata, and then the semicircular course round Begunder, Shooa, Amhara, and Damot, till it approaches within a day's journey of its sources. The regions which it chiefly watered were barbarous, and almost unknown; so, by an Abyssinian prince, who had marched an army into them, they were called the "New World." "Passing then," he says, "through innumerable regions and over stupendous precipices, it enters Egypt."

A long period elapsed before a European again visited Abyssinia, and the first to do so was James Bruce, then English Consul at Algiers. He explored Tripoli, Tunis, Syria, and Egypt; his object being to penetrate to the sources of the Nile, and in seeking to do this, he explored a great portion of the country, and displayed great resolution and perseverance in surmounting endless difficulties and dangers. Bruce left Massowah for the interior on November 10, 1769, and passing through Adowa, in Tigre, visited the monastery of Fremma, the chief establishment of the Jesuits. He describes it as about a mile in circumference, surrounded by walls flanked with towers, presenting the appearance of a castle rather than a convent.

He arrived at Gondar, the capital of Abyssinia, in February, 1770, where was the palace of the King. Here he ingratiated himself with the sovereign, and other influential persons, by professing to be a physician, courtier, and soldier.

He obtained permission to visit the sources of the Nile (Bahr-el-Azrek) which Payz claimed to have discovered. He visited first the great cataract of Alata, down which the Nile falls after passing through the Lake of Dembea. He describes it as the most magnificent sight he ever beheld. The whole river fell down in one sheet from the height of about 40 feet, with a force and noise which made our traveler dizzy. A thick haze covered the fall, and spread over the course of the stream both above and below.

Bruce had an interview at Bamba with Fasil, the Galla chief, who, with other confederates, had captured Gondar and set up a king of their own. At length he reached the district, a green and fertile region, in which those long-sought-for fountains were to be found. His emotions were first raised to the highest pitch by arriving at a portion of the infant stream so narrow that it could be stepped over, which he did in triumph, fifty or sixty times. He was led by his guide to the principal fountain. He now burst into raptures similar to those of Payz, at having arrived at an object which the most powerful sovereigns of ancient or modern times had sought in vain to explore.

Bruce quitted Gondar on December 26, 1771, and returned homewards by the route of Senaar, and arrived at the point of junction of the White and Blue Niles, near the spot where the city of Khartoum is now situated. He made the mistake of considering the Abyssinian Nile, the sources of which he had visited, as the true Nile, though he observes that the Bahr-el-Abiad rolls three times the volume of water and is constantly full, while the other is a great stream only in the rainy season. This theory has been disproved by the ge-

DESERT TRAVELER AND GUIDE.

ographer D'Anville, who showed conclusively, that the main stream of the Nile is the mighty river that flows through Equatorial Africa, having its rise in the great lake system discovered by Speke and Baker.

From here Bruce journeyed to Shendy, and pushing on to Berber, soon quitted the course of the river, which takes a great bend to the west. He and his companions traversed the great Nubian desert, where, for 500 miles, they met no human habitation. Only a few watering-places interrupted the expanse of naked rock and burning sands. The travelers had nearly sunk under this journey, especially as, towards the close of it, the camels were unable to proceed. He made, however, a last effort, by which they at length came in sight of the Nile, near Syene, where their sufferings terminated.

Bruce arrived at Alexandria early in March, 1773, whence he sailed for Marseilles, and proceeded to Paris, and thence to England, where he arrived in June, 1774, having been absent twelve years. He published, in 1790, a record of his travels. It met with a kind reception from the public, though there were critics who took exception to some of his statements, and insisted that he was unworthy of credence. Though there may have been exaggerations, the general truth of his facts have long since been established.

That Bruce considered he had discovered the sources of the great Nile instead of the lesser stream, was scarcely a subject of wonder considering the ignorance that existed in his day. After escaping great and manifold dangers in his wanderings through barbarous countries, this enterprising traveler lost his life in consequence of an accidental fall downstairs in his own house on April 26, 1794.

CHAPTER III.

Mungo Park's Travels.

In 1618, the African Company sent a vessel with the object of exploring the Gambia, commanded by Richard Thompson, with a cargo of goods to trade with the natives. Thompson proceeded as high up the river as Kassan; but the Portuguese, animated by jealousy, massacred most of the crew. It was subsequently learned that Thompson was murdered by his men.

The company did nothing in the way of discovery until 1723, when they sent another expedition to the Gambia; but it only proceeded 59 miles above Barraconda. While the English sought to ascend the Gambia, deeming it the Niger, the French navigated the Senegal, hoping to reach the city of Timbuctoo and the region of gold. At the mouth of this river they founded the settlement of Louis about the year 1625, and their director, General Brue, ascended the Senegal in the years 1697-98, reaching as high as Felu. He founded a fort called St. Joseph, which long continued the principal seat of French commerce on the Upper Senegal. Subsequent governors visited Bambouk; but the glories of African discovery in the regions of the Niger, as in those of Zambesi and the Equatorial lake region, were reaped by their English rivals.

Much of the success achieved was due to the African Association. Although the Company only offered their expenses to travelers who engaged to explore the interior of Africa, there were many eager aspirants for the honor. The first was Ledyard, who had circumnavigated the globe with Captain Cook, and lived for many years with the North American Indians. Ledyard, however, got no farther than Cairo, where he died in 1788. The next traveler engaged was Lucas, who had been three years a galley slave among the Moors, but he penetrated only a short distance from Tripoli. The third expedition was made by Major Houghton from a different quarter. He undertook to reach the Niger by the route of the Gambia, and not by boats, but by land. He set out early in 1791, and quitting the Gambia at Medina, arrived at Ferbanna on the Faleme. He pushed on, reached Timbuctoo, but was robbed and stripped, to wander about in the desert until he perished miserably,

Mungo Park, who long ranked as the chief of African travelers, was born on September 16, 1771, in Scotland. He received a good seminary education, and afterwards studied medicine at the University of Edinburgh. Having spent two years in London gaining the necessary qualifications, he set sail in May, and on June 21, 1795, arrived at Jillifree, near the mouth of the Gambia.

His instructions were to make his way to the Niger by Bambouk, or any other route, to ascertain the course of that river, and to visit the principal towns in its neighborhood, particularly Timbuctoo, and afterwards to return by way of the Gambia, or any other route he might deem advisable. Park at once proceeded up the Gambia to Pisania, where he set to work to learn the Madingo tongue, and to collect information from black traders. During his stay at Pisania, he was ill for two months with a severe fever, from which he recovered.

MUNGO PARK.

A caravan was about to start for the interior of Africa, and Park arranged to accompany it. He reached the town of Wassiboo, where he met eight fugitive Kaartan negroes, who had escaped from the Moors, and who were on their road to offer their allegiance to the King of Bambarra. Park agreed to accompany them. The near approach to Sego was indicated by the crowds hastening to its markets, and on July 21, 1796, one of his companions called out, "See the water!" and, looking forward, he says:—

"I saw with infinite pleasure the great object of my mission, the long-sought-for, majestic Niger, glittering in the morning sun, and flowing slowly to the east. I hastened to the brink, and having drunk of the water, lifted up my fervent thanks in prayer to the Great Ruler of all things for having thus far crowned my efforts with success." Sego, the capital of Bambarra, consists of four distinct towns; two on the north, and two on the south bank of the Niger, on which floated numerous canoes. The place is surrounded by high mud walls. The houses are built of clay, of a square form, with flat roofs, some of them of two stories, and most of them whitewashed. Moorish mosques are seen in every quarter, and the streets, though narrow, are broad enough for every useful purpose in a country where street carriages are unknown. Sego contains about 30,000 inhabitants.

He heard that Timbuctoo, the great object of his search, was entirely in possession of a savage and merciless band of Moors, who allowed no Christian to live there. He had advanced too far to think of returning, and determined to proceed.

Being provided with a guide, Park left the village on the morning of July 24, traveling through a cultivated country, the scenery resembling England more than he expected to find in the middle of Africa. In the even-

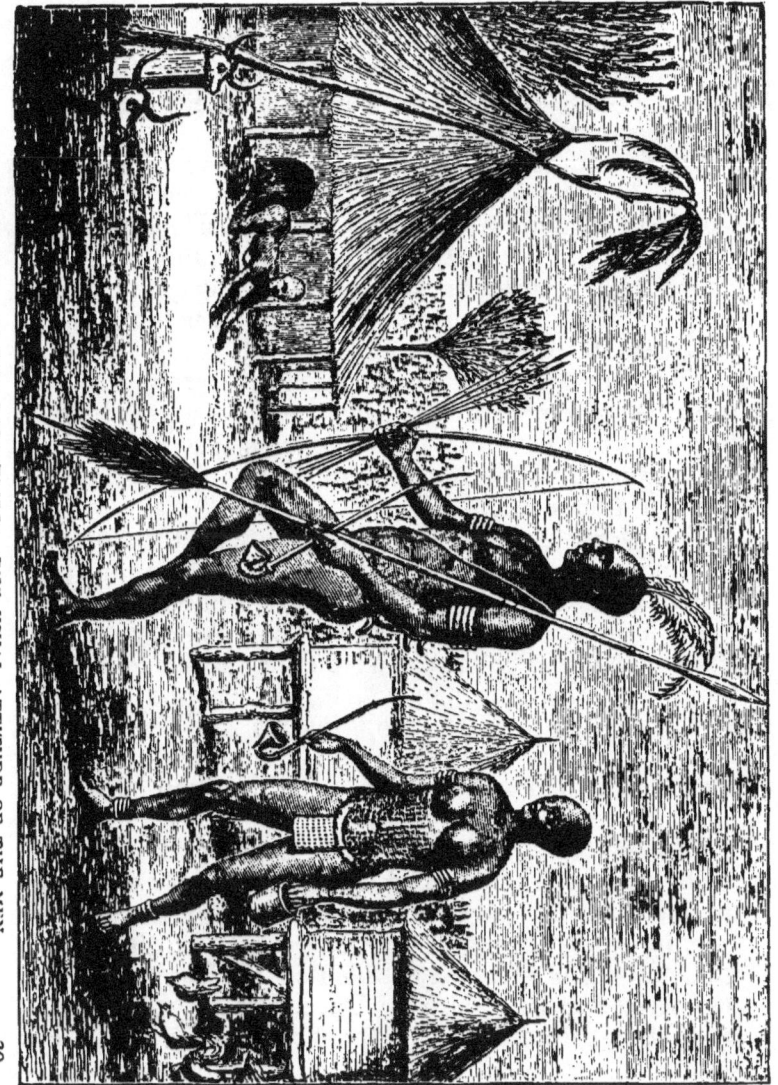

A HOMESTEAD OF THE BARI TRIBE: THE USUAL ATTITUDE OF THE MEN.

ing he reached the large town of Sansanding, the resort of numerous Moorish caravans from the shores of the Mediterranean.

On September 16, he reached the town of Kamalia, where he met a negro, Kafa Taura, who was collecting a caravan of slaves to convey to the European settlements on the Gambia, as soon as the rains should be over. Here Park was laid up by a fever, and passed five weeks in gloomy isolation. The fever left him in a very debilitated condition.

The caravan departed on April 19, 1797; and the irons being removed from the slaves, every one had his load assigned to him. Kafa had 27 slaves for sale, but eight others afterwards joined them. Altogether the caravan numbered 73 persons.

The worst part of the journey was through the Jallouka wilderness. The country was beautiful, and abounded with birds and deer, but so anxious were they to push on that they made 30 miles that day. Being advised that 200 Jalloukas were lying in wait to plunder them, they changed their course, and entered the town of Koba. On June 10, 1797, Pisania was reached, and Park was welcomed as one risen from the dead by his friends who had heard that the Moors had murdered him.

Park waited at Pisania some time, and finding no vessel likely to sail direct to England, he took his passage on board a slave vessel, bound for South Carolina. She, however, through stress of weather, put into Antigua, and from thence he sailed in an English packet, and arrived at Falmouth on December 22, 1797, having been absent from England about two years and seven months.

SLAVE HARDSHIPS.

(31)

Park published the narrative of his journey, early in 1799, and the interest attaching to his adventures made it very popular. After his return to England, Park married the daughter of Mr. Anderson, with whom he had served his apprenticeship as a surgeon, and resided a couple of years on the farm in Scotland.

After this he practised his profession for some time; but this sort of life not satisfying his ardent temperament, in October, 1801, he accepted an invitation made by the Government, to undertake an expedition, on a large scale, into the interior of Africa. Owing to the war with France, it was not until 1804, that he was authorized to make arrangements for the journey.

The expedition consisted of Park himself, his brother-in-law (Mr. Anderson), and George Scott, draughtsman, together with four artificers, who, on his arrival at Sego, were to build two boats, in which he purposed to sail down the Niger to the estuary of the Congo. Park sailed from Portsmouth on January 30, 1805, and after touching at the Cape Verde Islands, reached Goree on March 28. Here he selected 35 soldiers, under the command of Lieutenant Martyn, as well as two sailors from the *Squirrel*, a frigate.

On arriving at the Gambia, the party, full of hope and in high spirits, pushed on to Pisania. On May 4, the caravan set forth from Pisania, whence nearly ten years before Park had commenced his adventurous journey into the interior.

The arrangements for the march were well devised, but no human foresight could guard against the deadly influence of the African climate. One by one, in rapid succession, Park's companions were attacked by the fever. Some of them died; some were left behind on the road, and were no doubt robbed and murdered by the prowling thieves. Park himself, Scott, Martyn and Anderson were forced to give up, and stopped at some of the villages till they recovered sufficiently to resume their journey.

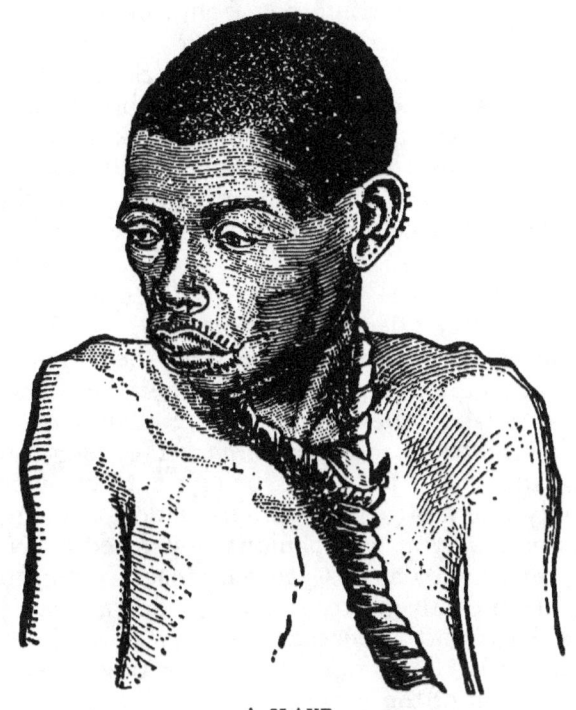

A SLAVE.

On August 19, the sad remnant of the expedition ascended the mountainous ridge which separates the Niger from the remote branches of the Senegal. Park hastened on ahead, and, coming to the brow of the hill, once more saw the mighty river. Descending from thence towards Bambakoo, the travelers pitched their tents under a tree near that town.

Of the 34 soldiers and four carpenters who left the Gambia, only six soldiers and one carpenter reached the Niger. All were suffering from sickness, and some nearly at the last extremity.

The sad news now reached him of Scott's death, and soon after his brother-in-law, Anderson, breathed his last. "No event," Park remarks, "which took place during the journey ever threw the smallest gloom over my mind, till I laid Mr. Anderson in the grave. I then felt myself left a second time lonely and friendless amidst the wilds of Africa."

Some days before this, the guide returned with a large canoe, much decayed and patched. Park and one of the surviving soldiers, took out all the rotten pieces, and, by adding on portions of another canoe, with 18 days' hard labor, they changed the Bambarra canoe into His Majesty's schooner *Joliba*. Her length was 40 feet, breadth six feet; and, being flat-bottomed, she drew only one foot of water when loaded. In this craft he and his surviving companions embarked on November 17, on which day his journal closes. He intended to begin his adventurous voyage down the Joliba. Besides Park and Lieutenant Martyn, two Europeans only survived. They purchased three slaves to assist in the navigation of the vessel.

Descending the stream, they passed Silla and Jenne without molestation; but lower down, in the neighborhood of Timbuctoo, they were followed by armed canoes, which they beat off, killing several of the natives. They had to fight their way down past a number of places, once striking on the rocks, and being nearly capsized by a hippopotamus which rose near them. Having a large stock of provisions, they were able to proceed without going on shore. At Yaour, the people threw lances and stones at him. He defended himself for a long time, till two of his slaves in the stern of the boat were killed.

Finding no hope of escape, Park took hold of one of the white men and jumped into the water, and Martyn did the same, hoping to reach the shore, but all were drowned in the attempt. The only slave remaining in the boat, seeing the natives persist in throwing their weapons, entreated them to stop. On this they took possession of the canoe and the man, and carried them to the King. From the interpreter was learned the manner in which Park and his companions had perished.

Park could not have been aware of the numerous rapids and other difficulties he would have to encounter in descending the upper courses of the Niger. In all probability his frail and ill-constructed vessel would have been wrecked before he had gone many miles below the spot where he lost his life. Had he succeeded in passing that dangerous part, he might have navigated the mighty stream to its mouth.

Although at first the account of Park's death was not believed in England, subsequent inquiries left no doubt that all the statements were substantially correct. Thus perished, in the prime of life, that heroic traveler, at the very time when he had good reason to believe that he was about to solve the problem of the Niger's course, and to dispel the belief that it was identical with the Congo. He died about the end of the year 1805.

CHAPTER IV.

Denham and Clapperton, and Oudney—Travels in the Great Sahara Borderland.

The dreadful termination to the wanderings and sufferings of Mungo Park in no way damped the ardor of British merchants for the extension of trade upon the Gambia, the Senegal, and the Niger; nor were geographers any the less inclined to push on inquiries eastwards from Senegambia and the Kong Mountains.

Park's life was not the first that had been sacrificed in those regions; his endeavors were not the only ones that had been partially futile. Richard Thompson went out in 1618, and died east of Kasson. Upon news of Park's decease being received, expeditions were launched, under Captain Tuckay and Major Peddie, the latter ascending the Congo to find its bearing, if any, upon the Niger, a doubt existing in many minds that the waters of the two rivers joined somewhere. As in Park's second enterprise, dysentery, fever, and death wrought fearful havoc and defeat, and subsequent exploration parties, headed by capable officers, did not accomplish very much more than confirming the discoveries of Houghton and Park, until a series of daring enterprises conducted by Captain Clapperton and Richard Lander added greatly to the knowledge concerning the rivers finding a limit upon the north-west coast of Africa, and in the discovery of Lake Tchad or Chad, 300 miles

HUGH CLAPPERTON.

in circumference, and in the regions of Bornou and Kassem—districts, like Songhay, Timbuctoo, and Sockatoo, centuries old, and whose history is very dimly recorded, notwithstanding the once mighty, well-organized rule of men.

Hugh Clapperton was a born explorer, of magnificent physique, and fearless in spirit; he sailed the Indian seas when a lad, was pressed into the navy, saw active service in Canada, and was affected by a desire to go out and fill in the gap left open by Mungo Park. Dr. Oudney, a personal friend of his, placed his services at the disposal of the Government for African exploration; and was appointed Consul to Bornou, with full permission to traverse the regions of North, Central, and Northwest Africa, and to take with him Captain Clapperton and Major Dixon Denham.

The course selected by Dr. Oudney was across the great Sahara. The desert was full of dangers, but the route was preferable for North Central African exploraation to any course from the west or from the Nile and the east.

The port of Tripoli was left behind in February, 1822, a caravan was constituted inland, and the town of Mourzak was reached with trifling loss.

A number of merchants swelled the caravan, and everything pointed to a successful march across the desert, which was duly completed, Kouka, upon the shores of Lake Tchad, and in the Bornou country, being reached February 7, 1823. Not, however, before every member of the united caravan had suffered greatly. Oudney and Clapperton were unwell at starting, and the terrible heat of the desert did not tend to improve their condition. Broad salt fields, glistening in the sun, had to be crossed; and we are told in Clapperton and Denham's account of their journeyings, how that, at irregular

THE DESERT—MIRAGE ON THE HORIZON.

intervals in the desert, skeletons of men, horses, and camels were to be seen. Human beings and animals had been overtaken by terrific sand-storms, or had survived them only to die of hunger and thirst. At one spot alone, nearly 100 skeletons were counted. They were but skeletons of blacks, carelessly exclaimed the Arabs, who laughed at the sympathy exhibited by the Englishmen. Large numbers were those of Soudanese captured for the slave market, and left to perish on the road to Fezzan, owing to the scarcity of provisions.

From Kouka expeditions were made, and much that was valuable geographically exposed. Denham went among the Mandara horsemen, and was robbed and stripped naked, as Park had been. Denham returned to Kouka, then went eastward, saw no more of Lake Tchad, and was back at Kouka, to welcome Clapperton from a journey into the Soudan region. Denham had started for the Soudan in company with Dr. Oudney in the middle of December, 1823. Joining a caravan, they passed among the Shooa Arabs, entered the city of Katagum, where they were received in state, and offered slaves as presents, and coming to Murmur, Oudney, who had healed many in these far-off towns and villages, and in the desert, was obliged himself to yield to the merciless inroads of consumption. He was buried in a deep grave by Clapperton, who was impelled to proceed to the walled trading city of Kano. He narrowly escaped death, fever attacking him. Three weeks later Clapperton was at Sockatoo, where he was received by the Sultan, from whose officers he learned something concerning poor Mungo Park's last days, and was told that the Niger flowed on to the sea at a place to the west, known as Jagra. Clapperton thereupon

A CARAVAN CROSSING THE DESERT.

resolved to follow the Niger, whose waters rolled on past Sockatoo.

At Bilma they laid in a stock of dates for the next 14 days, during which man and beast nearly subsisted upon them, the slaves for 20 days together mostly getting no other food.

Then came the stony desert, which the camels, already worn out by the heavy sand-hills, had to cross for nine days.

On the day they made El Wahr, and the two following, camels in great numbers dropped down and died, or were quickly killed and the meat brought in by the hungry slaves.

On January 21, 1825, they reached Tripoli, and soon after embarked for Leghorn, where they were long detained by quarantine, so that the three survivors of the expedition did not reach England till June 1, 1825, having been absent three years.

From the favorable report which Clapperton on his return home brought of the Sultan Bello of Sockatoo, and his wish to open up a commercial intercourse with the English, the Government determined to send out another expedition, in the hope that that object might be carried out, and that means might be found for putting a check on the slave trade in that part of Africa.

Clapperton, now raised to the rank of commander, was placed at the head of the expedition. Captain Pearce and a Mr. Morrison, a naval surgeon, were appointed to serve under him. He also engaged the services of Mr. Dickson, another surgeon, and of a very intelligent young man, Richard Lander, who was to act as his servant.

After a stay of only four months, Clapperton sailed

TRIPOLI.

from Portsmouth, and, touching at Sierra Leone, arrived at Benin on November 26, 1825.

Dickson, wishing to make his way alone to Sockatoo, was landed at Whidah, and set off for Dahomey. Here he was well received and set forward to a place called Shar, 17 days' journey from Dahomey. From thence he was known to have set forward with another escort, but from that time nothing whatever was heard of him.

At Benin, Clapperton met an English merchant who advised him not to ascend the river, but to take a route from Badagarry across the country to Katumga, the capital of Youriba. That the journey was an ill one was quickly shown, for fever and dysentery broke out, Pearce and Morrison being the first victims. Their death was a great blow to Clapperton; but like all explorers he was resolved, and he proceeded to the capital of Youriba, arriving there in the middle of January, 1826.

The Clapperton expedition struck the Niger at Boussa, the place of Park's death. Instead, however, of tracing its waters southwards, the direction in which it runs, the route was continued to Sockatoo. Report has it that a deadly aversion to sailing down the river or traversing its banks seized upon Clapperton, that a strong conviction took root in his mind, after viewing the scene of Park's tragic decease, that no white man would live to tell the story of the Niger outlet. Having stayed a short time at Sockatoo, Clapperton was preparing to leave when he was attacked by dysentery, and died April 13, 1827, yet one more victim to the Niger outlet fever.

Richard Lander tells the story of Clapperton's last days. The hero was aware that his end approached. Every day he would be carried into the open air and have read to him a portion of Scripture, particularly Psalm xcv. One day he called Lander into his wretched dwelling and said with calmness, " Richard, I shall soon be no more; I feel myself dying." Not long after that sad interview in the lonely hut, Clapperton breathed his last.

Having seen his master decently interred, and collected his papers and clothing, Richard Lander very pluckily led those remaining of the force to the coast by much the same route as that taken to Sockatoo. He would have trusted himself, young as he was, to the Niger, and discovered its outlet, had not the natives absolutely barred his progress.

Lander returned to Badagarry by the route which had been traversed by Clapperton, and reached London April 30, 1826.

Denham returned to Sierre Leone in 1826, as superintendent of the liberated Africans, and in 1828 he was appointed governor of the colony. On June 9, 1828, he died of a fever, after a few days' illness.

Denham and Clapperton made important contributions to the geography of Africa, though they failed in the chief object of their expedition to discover the course and connections of the Niger.

CHAPTER V.

The Landers: on the Banks of the Rolling Niger.

The achievment by Richard Lander was postponed. On his return home the probability of the Niger losing itself in the Atlantic was admitted, and to him was entrusted a mission to revisit, on behalf of the British Government, the town of Boussa. He was not to leave the Niger until its outlet should be determined, whether its disappearance was to the sea in the south-west, or eastwards to Lake Tchad; but to follow its course, if possible, to its termination, wherever that might be.

That voyage from Portsmouth to Cape Coast Castle, in the month of January, 1830, was surely the most remarkable, as regards the circumstances surrounding it, ever known.

Richard Lander was 26 years old. He had not the advantage of education upon his side. He was at sea, off to the West Indies, when a boy of twelve; and was in South Africa more than once while a lad, so that of scholarly attainments he could have none. His predecessors in North African exploration were versed in Arabic; Lander knew it not, nor anything worth the name of dialect. Of astronomy and navigation he could have a smattering, not more; while of medicine he was positively ignorant, and of trade he was as innocent.

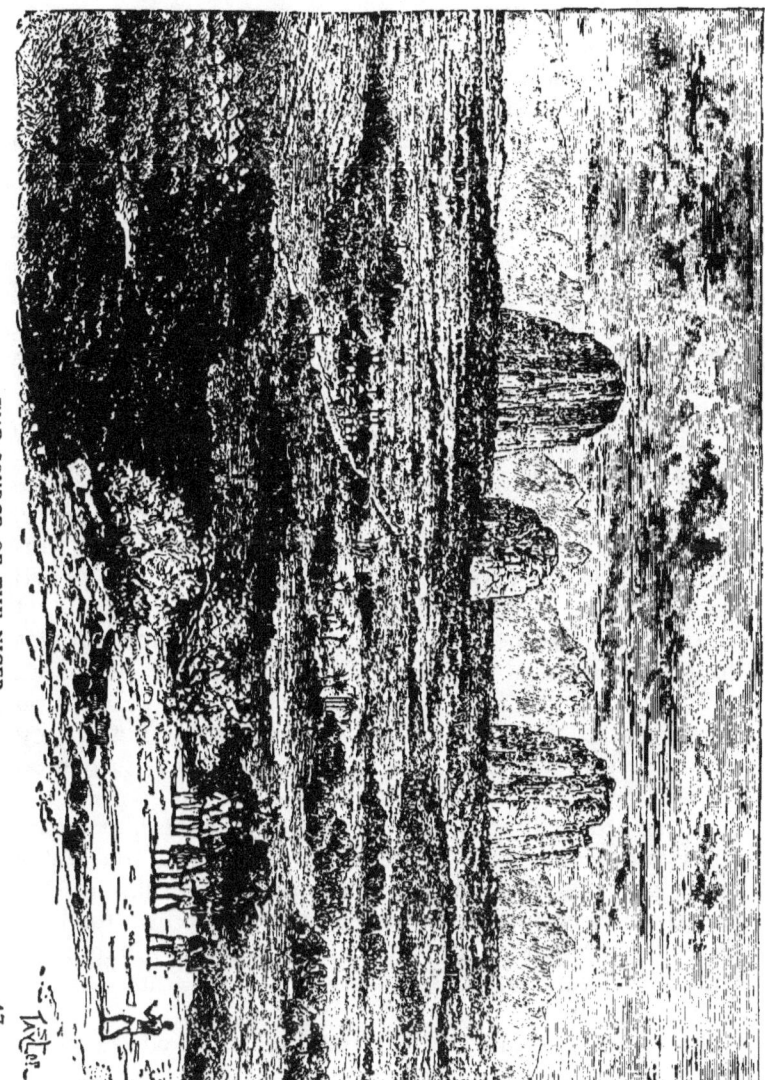

THE SOURCE OF THE NIGER.

Evidently he was imbued with courage—who else would have faced the dangers and fevers of the north-west coast territory, when so many able-bodied travelers had fallen a prey to their temerity?

Richard Lander possessed the qualities of a successful explorer. The courage, perseverance, and judgment exhibited by him in making his way from Sockatoo to the coast after the death of Clapperton, and the bold attempt to follow the course of the Niger to the sea, pointed him out to the Government as a fit person to lead another expedition with that object in view.

They went to Badagarry, and, on March 31, 1830, began their journey into the interior, proceeding up the river as far as it was navigable. Up country they procured horses, on which they continued their journey. Both the brothers suffered from sickness; but, undaunted, they pursued their course till they reached Katunga, the capital of Youriba.

Lander informed the King that his purpose was to go to Bornou by way of Youri, and requested a safe conduct through his territories. This permission was granted, and, sending their horses by land, they proceeded up the river in a canoe, which was furnished them, towards Youri.

After proceeding a short distance, the stream gradually widened to two miles, in some places the water being very shallow, but in others of considerable depth. Steering directly northward they voyaged on for four days, having passed, they were told, all the dangerous rocks and sand-banks which are to be found above Youri or below Boussa.

Landing at a little village on the bank, where their

horses met them, they rode a distance of eight miles to the walls of Youri.

Their visit to the Sultan of Youri was not without interest, as it enabled them to obtain the only relics of the last journey of Mungo Park that have ever come to light. These were a richly embroidered robe, a gun, an old nautical almanac, a book of the Psalms of David, and his journal,* describing his journey from the Gambia to the Niger.

The King expressed his readiness to assist them, but declared that he could not forward them on their way to the eastward, as he would be unable to guarantee their safety, and that the best thing he could do was to send them back to Boussa.

On August 2, they set off on their road to Boussa, but here they were kept some weeks.

It was September 30 before they obtained the canoes, and were able to embark. The current rapidly bore them down the stream. Their voyaye began prosperously; but they were detained at several places by the chiefs, who wished to get as much as they could out of them.

At Leechee the Niger was found to be three miles in width. The boatmen they engaged here paddled on

* With this journal was the following letter from the heroic traveler, addressed to Lord Camden, dated, " On board H. M. schooner *Joliba*, at anchor off Sansandig, November 17, 1805.—I have turned a large canoe into a tolerably good schooner, on board of which I this day hoisted the British flag, and set sail with the fixed resolution to discover the termination of the Niger, or perish in the attempt. . . . . My dear friend Mr. Anderson, and likewise Mr. Scott, are both dead : but, though all the Europeans who are with me should die, and though I were myself half dead, I would still proceed, and if I could not succeed in the object of my journey, I would at least die on the Niger." This heroic resolve the great traveler sealed a few days later with his life.

for forty minutes, refused to go farther, and they had to wait till they could obtain a fresh crew. Indeed, at the different places at which they stopped, they were vexatiously delayed on various pretexts by the natives.

A palaver with King Obie of Brass Town had an unpleasant sequel. Near as the Landers were to the sea, they were to be disposed of as slaves, they were informed secretly. Provisions could scarcely be procured, there were renewed threats of detention; and more attacks of fever made the situation most depressing. The brothers were prisoners without any prospect of freedom.

Richard Lander had nothing to offer; he and John were reduced to poverty and wretchedness. Only one condition they could propose—that, given their liberty, any tax or ransom fixed upon by the sable chief, would be forthcoming the moment they arrived within the sphere of British influence. That promise the brothers faithfully discharged.

Richard Lander, leaving his brother as hostage and his men at the town, set off in a canoe that was to convey him to the sea. After traveling 60 miles down the river, his feelings of delight may be imagined when he had ocular evidence that he had at length succeeded in tracing the mysterious Niger down to the ocean, by seeing before him two vessels, one the Spanish slaver, the other an English brig.

The chief was induced to go back to bring John Lander and the rest of the men on Richard's reiterated promise that he would obtain the goods they had promised him. He took passage on the English brig for Rio Janeiro, which they reached on March 16, and from there obtained a passage to England, which they reached safely on June 10, 1831.

Thus with very humble means, by the energy and courage of two unpretending men, was the long-disputed problem of the course of the Niger to the sea completely solved—a discovery for long years denied to older and more experienced men.

The Royal Geographical Society awarded to Richard Lander their gold medal and a money prize of fifty guineas.

The discoveries disclosed by the Landers quickened the desire for further extension of trade upon the northwest coast of Africa and to towns far inland, and Richard Lander embarked July 25, 1832, to act from the mouth of the river whose possibilities were now partially understood. It was a difficult enterprise; more serious than the merchants who commissioned Lander imagined. He got many miles inland, to the banks of the Tchadda, a tributary to the Niger, it will be remembered; was beaten back by superior numbers, tried again, was forced to escape coastwards, and he ascended the Niger from the ocean a third time. It was his last effort. He was attacked, wounded by a poisoned arrow, and from its effects he expired, February 6, 1834.

CHAPTER VI.

Explorations of Dr. Barth in Central Africa.

The British Government had, in 1849, appointed James Richardson, an experienced traveler in Africa, to the command of an expedition which was to start from Tripoli, and thence endeavor to penetrate to the central part of the continent. Dr. Barth, who had spent three years traveling through Barbary and the desert tracts to the westward bordering the shores of the Mediterranean, was allowed, accompanied by another German, Dr. Overweg, to join the expedition. A light boat, which was divided into two portions and could be carried on the backs of camels, was provided, and a sailor to navigate her either on Lake Tchad or down the Niger.

One of the principal objects of the expedition was the abolition of the slave trade, which it was known was carried on to a fearful extent in those regions. The principal employment of the Moorish tribes on the borders of the territories inhabited by blacks was still, as in the days of Mungo Park and Clapperton, slave-hunting. Villages were attacked for the purpose, when the prisoners captured were carried northward across the desert and sold in Morocco and the other Barbary states.

Another object was the opening up a lawful commercial intercourse with the people who might be visited, and the exploration of the country for scientific purposes, as well as to discover the course of the great river which the Landers had seen flowing into the Niger in their adventurous voyage down that stream.

Dr. Barth was the man to succeed. That success stamps him as a true hero; no individual save one with all the qualities of heroism could or would have passed through the perils he experienced. He started with Richardson and Dr. Overweg in 1849 to explore the forbidding Sahara and parts of Central Africa. Richardson, the leader of the expedition, arrived safely at Mousak, Tripoli, branched due west to a point near Ghat, and wandered hither and thither, north and south. On March 4, 1851, Richardson fell a victim to fatigue, and 18 months afterwards Dr. Overweg expired in the region between Sockatoo and Lake Tchad. Practically alone, and his ardor for exploration unabated, Barth left no place of importance west of Lake Tchad and east of Sockatoo, and on the southern banks of the lake untouched, striking the Niger at a point south of the latter place, and some miles north of Boussa. To him is owing the discovery of the Binue, the largest affluent of the Niger. News came to England of the deaths of Richardson and Overweg, and the worst was feared regarding Barth. In the early part of 1853, a relief force was despatched, which reached the banks of the Tchad. Not to meet Barth, however, who returned across the Sahara without coming in contact with his would-be rescuer, after a course of travel quite unique.

The route of Richardson, Barth, and Overweg was

through the Fezzan country from Tripoli. They had more than the average amount of luggage, which gave them great trouble. A steel boat carried in two sections, for use upon Lake Tchad, proved cumbersome in the extreme, until divided into four parts distributed more evenly among the camels of the caravan. South of Mouzak, Barth was literally lost in the desert. Anxious to ascend a mountain he left the caravan without a guide, hoping to follow in its track, and come up with it. But his excitement took him on too far. Having satisfied his curiosity he gazed around, hungry, thirsty, footsore and overheated; but there was nothing to indicate the course he ought now to pursue. He was harried in every direction, sinking sometimes in soft dry sand, firing his rifle the while in the hope that his friends would learn of his whereabouts and await his coming. To no purpose. Darkness fell upon the desert with Barth a solitary wanderer in it, and so exhausted, mentally and physically was he, that the sight of a number of large fires in the distance served but to bring laments instead of serving to cheer him. He could not move a step farther. Fever came upon him, and he could not sleep, he fired again, but to no purpose, morning broke, and the sun rising higher and higher in the heavens, his situation was pitiful in the extreme. Just as he was resigning himself to what he believed would be his last sleep, he was aroused by a mounted Arab who had tracked him, and stretching out his hands for help, had the pleasure of being relieved by water from the skin carried by the camelman. He was assisted by him to the caravan a few miles away.

Barth's providential escape served to sharpen his desire for further adventure, for when eight miles from

Sellufet, in the desert region, he set out upon a bullock to the old and partially decayed town of Agades, and surprised the Sultan, as the first white man his majesty had beheld. Barth was two months absent from the caravan, rejoined it, left it again on the south-western confines of the Soudan; thence passing through a well-cultivated country, and among smiling homesteads, he arrived at Kano, in Haussa, about equally distant between Sockatoo and Lake Tchad. Kano is a city of much importance, a centre for trade among the owners of caravans from the north, south, east and west, and a resting-place for those eager for repose after passing amid the difficulties of travel in Northern Africa. Barth reckoned upon a fair reception, but he arrived in a reduced condition, presents to chiefs and princes having considerably lessened his stock of goods. He was astonished to see the extent of the city, its large, well-built houses, its trading establishments, the briskness of its commerce, its workshops and the superior, even elegant, fashions of dress among the free men and women. But the Moors are in large numbers in Kano, and this fact speaks volumes. At Kouka, again, Barth found it as Clapperton had done, a city of more than 50,000 souls, engaged more or less in trade and commerce, and living in houses and amid surroundings quite equal to those obtaining in Kano. It was at Kouka that Barth heard of Richardson's death. The latter died in the city some weeks prior to the doctor's arrival. Overweg came in subsequent to a flying visit paid by Barth to Lake Tchad, and the two started for exploration in the south, moved in towns and villages notorious for their systems of slavery, went to the eastern shores of Lake Tchad, were attacked and plundered by Arabs, and had a ripe experience in the Mandara country. At Kouka once more, in February, 1852, the two parted—Overweg to visit Lake Tchad, Barth to go to the Begharmi country.

Some tribes of Arabs had rebelled against the Turks, and he was in some danger while in their hands. Escaping from them, he reached Tripoli in the middle of August, and arrived safely in London on September 6, 1855.

Although much of the country he had passed over was already known, no previous African traveler more successfully encountered and overcame the difficulties and dangers of a journey through that region.

The most important result of his adventurous journey was the discovery of a large river, hitherto unknown, falling into Lake Tchad from the south, and of the still larger affluent of the Niger, the Binue, which, rising in the far-off centre of the continent, flows through the province of Adamawa.

The courage and perseverance of Dr. Barth, while for five years traveling 12,000 miles, amidst hostile and savage tribes, in an enervating climate, frequently with unwholesome or insufficient food, having ever to keep his energies on the stretch to guard himself ·from the attack of open foes or the treachery of pretended friends, have gained for him the admiration of all who read his travels, and place him among the foremost of African travelers.

CHAPTER VII.

DISCOVERIES OF CAPTAINS BURTON AND SPEKE IN CENTRAL AFRICA.

RICHARD BURTON, better known as a traveler by the name of Captain Burton, may be regarded as the *doyen* of African travelers. Burton's discovery of Lake Tanganyika in 1857, started the race for Central African exploration, in which he was followed by his fellow-traveler on that occasion, Speke, the discoverer of Lake Victoria Nyanza, by Grant, the companion of Speke, by Samuel Baker, and by Stanley, the " Prince of African travelers," as Burton acknowledged him to be.

Captain Burton's name was already familiar to the public, especially in India, by his adventurous journey to Mecca, where, in the character of one of " the faithful," he worshipped at the Kaaba, the shrine of Mahomet, in the eyes of every Mussulman the most sacred spot on earth. Burton's adventures on this memorable journey had made him a notable man when he undertook the exploration of Somaliland, and his pen had already found congenial occupation in writing an account of the newly acquired province of Scinde, where he had served under Napier.

Besides being, perhaps, the most eminent linguist of his age—he was more or less familiar, we believe, with twenty-five languages of Europe, Asia and Africa—he has explored many parts of East and West Africa. He was the author of numerous books of travel, and was distinguished as an archæologist and man of letters, as his work on Etruria, and his translations of Camoens, and of "The Thousand and One Nights," prove. Sir Richard Burton was one of the most remarkable men of his day, and his many-sidedness is shown in his physical acquirements, no less than in the points indicated above. He is noted as an accomplished swordsman, and his book on the sword is a standard work. Altogether, we may regard him as a veritable "admirable Crichton." He had served in the Indian army, and was regarded as a reliable and able officer. Little was known of the Somali when he was selected to explore their country from Berbera, opposite Aden.

Burton's companion in his expedition was John Hanning Speke. His career from his 18th year was one continuous round of strange and extremely perilous adventure. Born in 1827, he went to India at the age of 17, as a lieutenant in the British army, and served in a number of general actions. The desperate hazard of war was not enough for the uneasy, daring, roving spirit of Speke—he must wander into mysterious Thibet, climb the great lonely Himalayas, and explore country, whenever he could obtain leave, in the intervals of peace allowed to the English troops in India in those days.

The enterprise of seeing the towering snow-capped Mountains of the Moon, Kilimandjaro and Keina, was exactly the thing to suit Speke's taste. Captain Burton having received a commission from the Government of India to explore the country of the Somalis, in

RICHARD BURTON.

Northeast Africa, and bounded partly by the Gulf of Aden, Speke obtained permission to join him.

Burton, Speke, and two other Europeans of the party, Lieutenants Stoyan and Herne, were soon to learn the character of some of the natives, in an unpalatable fashion. Hardly had they located themselves near Berbera, when, in the dead of night, they were set upon by a body of marauders, the animals bought for caravan purposes were taken, while Speke was made captive, Stroyan was brutally murdered; Burton and Herne escaping without injury. Speke eluded his captors, and running for the sands upon the Gulf of Aden, he and his companions were rescued by a passing boat on her way to the port of Aden.

The expedition to the Somali country having been formally recalled, Speke hastened to the Crimea. The war was then drawing to a close, and he had no opportunity to test the strength of Russian steel. It happened, as he desired—he was permitted to associate himself with the force fitting for exploration in Southeast Africa, taking in the Mountains of the Moon. A broad and magnificent lake had been spoken of by natives and Arab traders, and Captain Burton, given the lead of the party, was empowered to inquire, explore, and report, as to whether the report was correct or otherwise. On December 21, 1856, Burton and Speke landed at Zanzibar; not, however, until May, 1857, was the expedition fairly launched; the rainy season and illnesses caused inconvenience and delay.

The objective was Ujiji. It was believed then that the town was at the southern end of the great central lake, supposed by the way, to be 800 miles long by 350 broad

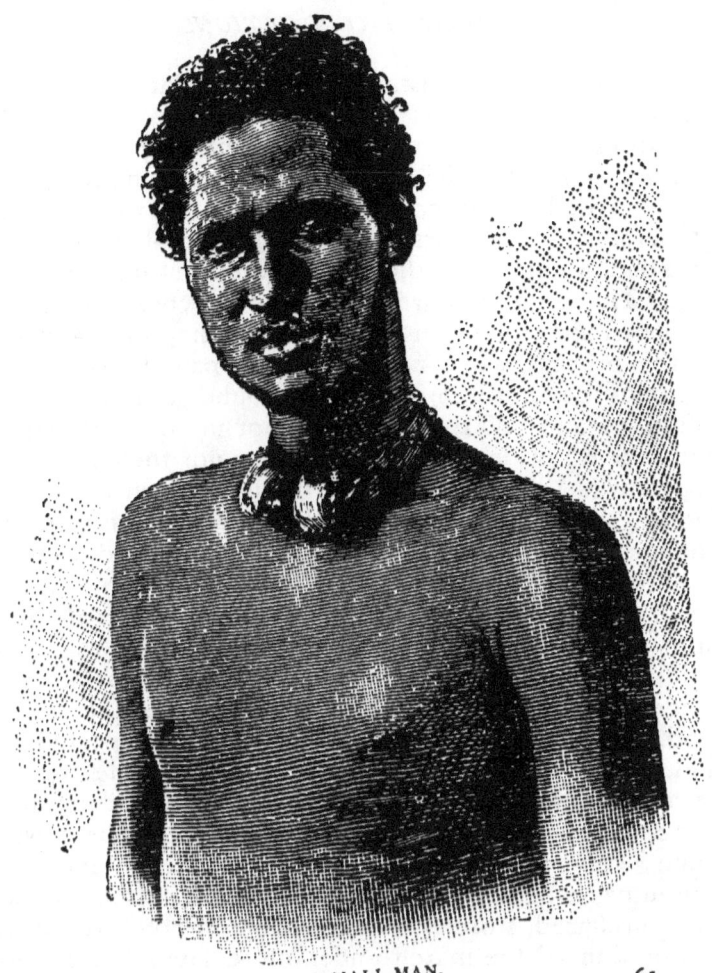

SOMALI MAN.

—wofully under the estimates made at later times, as we shall presently see.

Through the lands of the Wazaramo, the Wakhuta, and, extraordinary feature among African natives, the long-bearded Waziraha, proceeded the caravan to Zungomero. The Wazaramo lived in small huts, surrounded, a number of them together, by strong palisading. The men and women bestow devoted attention to their hair, twisting it tightly, and using clay and oil in the process, while no attention is paid to shielding the body beyond wearing a cloth round the loins. The Wakhuta and Waziraha are inferior in some respects, and take no pride in their dwellings, nor their personal appearance. Slavery prevails, though not in its worst forms. West of Zungomero, the aspect of the country changes—at one time hot springs rise from sandy plains, at another there are swamps in which the dregs of fever lie, as Burton and Speke found to their cost, a number of native porters succumbing, while Burton himself was stricken and could only journey on in great pain. To render matters worse, carriers begun a dispute as to food, and at one place where the leaders expected to find a good supply of necessaries, not a particle was to be picked up—slave-hunters had been busy and literally ruined the village by fire and kidnapping. There was some compensation for the travelers, however, at Rumuma, where caravans were wont to stop. Food was purchased, stores were replenished, and there was a resumption of the march under more favorable conditions, until the Usagara mountain ranges were practically left behind, and rest was obtained in Ugogo.

Men and animals were by this time thoroughly fagged out. Burton was far from well, and Speke was prostrated. Still, the halt was not a long one—a party of Unyamenzi were starting for their homes after serving as porters, and as those homes were within easy distance of the Mountains of the Moon, the opportunity of profiting by the presence of these men was not to be lost. They were conversant with the route from Ugogo, and had information to impart as to the wonderful snow-clad mountains. A start was made in the desired direction, which took the explorers through Unyamyembe, where Stanley and Livingstone were to part 15 years afterwards. Burton and Speke were imposed upon by petty chiefs until Tura was reached, when a fulsome reception was accorded them.

The caravan pushed on, and in September the Unyamenzi country, embracing the Mountains of the Moon, was actually reached. It is charming in parts, well wooded mounds and fertile valleys being conspicuous—villages lie clustered "above the impervious walls of milk-bush with its coral-shaped arms, and in rich pasture lands graze extensive herds of plump, high-humped cattle." Speke thinks that Unyamenzi must have been one of the largest kingdoms in Africa. He refers to the people as hereditarily the greatest traders in the continent, and as the only people who for love of barter and change will leave their own country as porters and go to the coast. "The whole country ranges nearly 4000 feet above the sea level. The natives are generally industrious, cultivate extensively, make cloths of cotton in their own looms, smelt iron, and work it up very expertly, and keep flocks and herds to a considerable extent. Some of the men are handsome and the women pretty."

At Kaze, in December, Burton and Speke were soon

mixing among the Arab merchants who make the town a caravan centre. Offers of help were made to the Englishmen, and some valuable information was gleaned. Our travelers were assured that Ujiji was not upon the southern end of the great lake of which they were really in search—that it did not stand upon the lake. The vast sheet they desired to explore was farther north, and from it ran a river flowing north again. This was news indeed. Another wonder. What solution? Burton and Speke had no definite idea then that the "farther lake" was the Victoria Nyanza, and that the "river" flowing north was none other than the mighty Nile, whose sources had been for long centuries a secret to geographers, and the search for which was to cost Livingstone so tremendous an amount of trouble and eventually his very life.

Increasingly curious as to the developments of the future, the explorers left Kaze after a stay of three weeks' duration—only to be mortified, however, by mutiny among the carriers, by the desertion of a number of those men they were depending upon to assist them in the selection of route, and by inability, for a season, to obtain others. The eyes of the leaders were seriously affected, and, for a week Burton lay prostrated by an illness that threatened his existence. The dawn of the year 1858 was a sad one; notwithstanding the travelers were marching past the bases of what they believed to be those mountains, word of which had prompted them to start upon their journeyings.

February 13, 1858, was to be a red-letter day, alike for the expedition and in the history of geographical discovery. Burton had mounted the summit of a rocky eminence, when his heart leaped—he beheld the water

A VIEW TAKEN AT UJIJI.

of Tanganyika. In the first place his gaze filled him with dismay, he records; the remains of his blindness, the veil of trees, and a broad ray of sunshine illuminating but one reach of the lake, had shrunk its fair proportions. Somewhat prematurely he began to curse his folly in having risked life and lost health for so poor a prize, and to propose a return to the coast. But advancing a few yards, the whole scene burst upon his view, filling him with admiration, wonder, and delight. Nothing, in sooth, could be more picturesque than this first view of Tanganyika Lake, as it lay in the lap of the mountains in the gorgeous tropical sunshine, its clear waters gleaming against a background of steel-colored mountains." To Speke the magnificent spectacle and the thrill of delight were denied. He was not far from Burton, but was suffering from inflammation of the eyes, his vision was dimmed, he was the only one in the throng standing within the shadows of what they regarded as the Mountains of the Moon, who could not look upon their imposing slopes nor yet upon the waters of the vast lake. An amount of keen disappointment would have been saved to Speke, had he known that the exploration party were not standing anywhere near the Mountains of the Moon. These grand, snow-capped giants are much farther north; they are east-southeast of the then undiscovered Victoria Lake—not rising from the eastern shores of Tanganyika. The explorers scarcely realized their true position.

Boats for the conveyance of the party to Kanele, in the Ujiji district, were obtained; but their reception, though pleasing, was followed by the extortions of the chief Kannina and his refusal of help towards procuring a boat, that the great lake might be explored. A month was wasted, in an unsuccessful attempt to hire an Arab sailing vessel, and it was not until many more days had elapsed that two wretched canoes were obtained; for which an exorbitant price had to be paid. With them went the chief Kannina. He knew something of a river flowing from the mountains into the lake, and would show it to them. He refused to continue in their company after the arrival at Uvira, at the north-east end of the lake—the Warundi regarded him as an enemy, and he feared to provoke their hostility.

All the searching and all the inquiries made by Burton and his followers yielded nothing to their view in the shape of a river. They were now at the farthest point traders were permitted to touch—beyond was a country of savages among whom it was advisable not to venture. Provisions were short, and the means of barter, and the presents were running out. The order was given, therefore, for a return to Ujiji.

On May 13, Burton and Speke were back at Ujiji, whence a return was made to Kaze, and Speke, accompanied by 10 Beloochs and 20 carriers, set out in search of the second lake, concerning which information had been given by Arabs and traders. Burton was so ill that he had to me carried from Ujiji to Kaze, and at the latter place he remained during Speke's absence north It was a journey beset with trials of patience—bad conduct on the part of the porters, detention by petty chiefs, and, by no means least, a detour and a long suspense in the new lake region, owing to the prevalence of bitter war.

But the daring and faith of Speke were to be rewarded. He was certain, before the end of July arrived, that he was approaching another great inland sea; and on August 3, his eyes were gladdened and his senses quickened by the vast expanse of the blue waters of the Nyanza or lake, bursting suddenly upon his gaze. He had seen its waters, as a fact, on July 30, but in narrow creeks.

Speke, in his book of travels, says: "The pleasure of the mere view vanished in the presence of those more intense and exciting emotions which were called up by the consideration of the commercial and geographical importance of the prospect before me. I no longer felt any doubt that the lake at my feet gave birth to that interesting river -the source of which has been the subject of so much speculation and the object of so many explorers. The lake is so broad you could not see across it, and so long that nobody knew its length." The breadth was estimated at 100 miles—as Speke remarks, no one had any idea of its length, more than one native seemed to think its termination in the north was in the end of the earth. Speke was forced to make his way back to Burton without obtaining any conception of the area of this the largest inland sea of Africa. People at home could scarcely credit Speke's account and estimate of this vast lake when he recited them—a lake to which he gave the name of "Victoria," in honor of the Queen of England.

Extraordinary, however, as Speke's opinion of the Victoria Nyanza seemed, it was no exaggeration. Much as he saw, and great as was his estimate of areas unseen, what he has stated has actually fallen below the mark. Subsequent travelers have sailed its waters and explored its banks, but even they have had an inadequate notion of its vastness. It has been left to Stanley to give us a more correct idea of the tremendous extent of this lake.

NAVIGATION ON LAKE TANGANYIKA.

Thirty years after its discovery by Speke, he passed its southern limits in the company of Emin Pasha, after bringing him from the Equatorial province, and says, he and his companions then made an unexpected discovery of real value in Africa of a considerable extension of the Victoria Nyanza to the south-west. The utmost southerly reach of this extension is south latitude 20° 48', which brings the water within 155 miles from Lake Tanganyika. No one had ever a suspicion of this before. He made a rough sketch of it, and found that the area of the lake was increased by this the latest discovery to 26,900 square miles, or just 1900 square miles larger than the reputed exaggerations of Captain Speke. An inconceivably wonderful lake, and having possibilities we are quite unable to understand!

Speke rejoined Burton at Kaze, August 28, and reported to him his momentous discovery. Circumstances prevented a return to the Victoria Nyanza, and a six months' march was begun to the coast, Zanzibar being the limit reached.

Again in England, Burton and Speke were the lions of the season, and their discoveries formed the main theme for geographers for many a day. To Burton were awarded the gold medals of the English and French Geographical Societies. In the following year he was appointed British Consul in Fernando Po. On October 20, 1890, he closed his varied and eventful career.

Lady Burton, in the "life" of her husband, says: "Burton was the pioneer (without money, without food, without men, or proper escort, without the bare accessaries of life, to dare and do, in spite of every obstacle, and every crushing thing, bodily and mentally), who opened up that country. It is to *him* that later followers, that Grant, and Speke, and Baker, and Stanley, and all the other men that have ever followed, owe it that he opened the oyster shell for them, and they went in to take the pearl. I don't want to detract from any other traveler's merits, for they are all brave and great, but I *will* say that if Richard Burton had had Stanley's money, escort, luxuries, porterage, and white comrades, backed by influence, there would not have been one single white spot on the whole map of the great Continent of Africa that would not have been filled up.

"It was the first successful attempt to penetrate that country, and laid the foundation for others. It was the base on which all subsequent journeys were founded; Livingstone, Cameron, Speke and Grant, Baker and Stanley carried it out. During these African explorations he was attacked with fever 21 times, by temporary paralysis, and partial blindness. Tanganyika was Burton's discovery. Nyanza was Speke's."

CHAPTER VIII.

SPEKE AND GRANT AT THE SOURCES OF THE NILE.

SPEKE could not rest in England. His adventurous spirit was in no sense subdued by the vicissitudes he had met among mountain passes of India and Thibet, upon the Somali plains, in the Crimea, and in connection with three years' exploration in South-east Africa; he was convinced that what he had seen of the Victoria Nyanza and in the country of the Mountains of the Moon was but a tithe of what might be gleaned thereabouts. There were, he felt sure, immense openings arising from a resumption of travel in those regions—elements to lead men on to sustained discoveries of greatest importance. The scheme Speke had cherished of traveling to the sources of the Nile and following it to its very outlet far away in North Africa was not forgotten by him. And he determined that at all costs he would reduce his convictions to the test. If no public body would help him, he would go out at his own expense as he originally intended, pursue his way, and come out victorious, or—perish in the endeavor.

Speke was not to launch his enterprise unsupported. Roderick Murchison was President of the Geographical Society, and his active sympathy was enlisted. The theory of Captain Speke (he had been promoted in the

DEPARTURE OF CAPTAINS SPEKE AND GRANT

British Army) that the Nile took its rise in the Victoria Nyanza, was favored by many, and they were very anxious that it should be thoroughly established. Nine months elapsed before he left the shores of England, as leader of the new expedition. He was somewhat disappointed in the amount of money voted him— $12,500,—and in his voyage to Zanzibar. He could not obtain passage thither at the time fixed by him— he and an old friend, Captain Grant, who was to accompany him inland, had to take the West African coast route to the Cape, and to sail thence for the port of debarkation. The time was not wholly lost, however. Speke received carbines, ammunition, and instruments from the Government at home, and, while at the Cape, a sum of $1500 was set apart by Parliament there for the purposes of the expedition, and ten Hottentot members of the Mounted Rifles were placed at his disposal, as well as a corvette for the shipment of his party to Zanzibar. On the way there the vessel chased and overtook a slave ship, in which were 500 poor blacks, who were released, when opportunity offered.

Speke and Grant left Zanzibar in August 1860, and the start eastwards was made from Bagomoyo. Provisions and articles for presents to native potentates were borne in plenty by the blacks. Eleven mules and five asses were taken for carrying purposes also. Very soon the force was reduced by sickness and desertion, and the gaps could not be filled without much trouble and provocation. There were 54 Wanguana freed-men, and about 20 Zanzibaris as porters, in addition to the Hottentots.

The march was through the flat country of Uzaramo,

through uneven stretches of Usagara, Ugogo, and Unyameuzi, until Lake Victoria was touched upon its

THE KING ADDRESSING HIS SUBJECTS.

south-western limits. Experiences passing through were not of the happiest. There were greedy chiefs to satisfy, porters mutinied and deserted, natives were suspicious, because they had the impression a slave-raiding caravan was approaching; guides were not to be trusted, porters were deceived and robbed, and in one village an illness contracted by Speke nearly proved fatal. Grant was then at some distance making observations and confirming native reports, and before rejoining Speke his escort was attacked, stripped of their loads, and put to flight. A few only of the loads were recovered.

But compensation was in store for the travelers who had now been fighting against nature, and often against savages, for twelve months. Speke and Grant left Usai behind and crossed into Karagwe, upon the western shores of the Victoria Lake, to find it a land of milk and honey. It contained a hitherto undiscovered lake, to which Speke gave the name of Little Windermere. Upon the very borders of Karagwe the badly-used, reduced explorers were met by messengers sent by Rumanika, the king, to accord them hearty welcome, and to offer them the best food and liquor in the land.

Speke says, "To do royal honors to the king of this charming land, I ordered my men to put down their loads and fire a volley. Here we saw, sitting cross-legged upon the ground, Rumanika and his brother Nnanaji, both of them men of noble appearance and size. The king was plainly dressed in an Arab's black choga, and wore for ornament, dress stockings of rich-colored beads, and neatly-worked wristlets of copper. At their sides lay huge pipes of black clay. The king and his brother had fine oval faces, large eyes and high noses, denoting the best blood of Abyssinia." The curiosity of the monarch as to how the explorers had found their way into his kingdom had to be satisfied, time flying "like magic" until the shades of evening fell and royalty and visitors separated, the latter to choose their own camping-ground amid charming scenery.

Throughout a month's intercourse with Rumanika, Speke experienced nothing save pleasure. Hunting, exploring, inquiring into the customs of the people, resting, day succeeded day all too quickly. When, however, a message came from the mighty Mtesa, king of Uganda, in January (1862), that he would receive the travelers, and the protection of Arab traders could be had, Speke was compelled to bid good-bye to Rumanika and his well-disposed people. Grant was too ill to be moved. After the lapse of a month, Speke neared Mtesa's capital. Like Rumanika, he sent couriers to welcome the explorer, and to promise to make him comfortable.

Speke's first view of the capital presented a magnificent sight—a whole hill was covered with gigantic huts such as he had never seen in Africa before. "I prepared for my first presentation at court," says Speke in his account of the reception by Mtesa, "though I cut a sorry figure in comparison with the display of the dressy Waganda. They had head-dresses, and were rich in ornaments. A number of the four hundred wives kept by Mtesa stood in little groups gazing upon us. Courtiers of high dignity stepped forward to greet me, dressed in the most scrupulously neat fashions. Men, women, bulls, dogs, and goats were led about by strings; cocks and hens were carried in men's arms; and little pages, with rope-turbans, rushed about, conveying messages, as if their lives depended on their swiftness, everyone holding his skin cloak tightly round him lest his naked legs might by accident be shown.

"The mighty king was sitting on his throne. He was a good-looking, well-figured, tall young man of twenty-five, sitting on a red blanket spread upon a square platform of royal grass, encased in tiger-grass reeds. The hair of his head was cut short, excepting on the top, where it was combed up into a high ridge, running from stem to stern like a cockscomb. The king wore many ornaments, principally of brass and copper. He was very affable and our interview was very satisfactory."

Speke appears to have taken Mtesa's fancy. Probably his presents had much to do with it. A healthy spot was fixed upon for Speke's abode, food in plenty was set apart for him, and on many days Mtesa accompanied him on hunting expeditions. So fond, indeed, was the king of Speke, that he would not hear of him leaving his dominions, and for more than four months our hero was compelled to stay in the neighborhood of the court. All was not pleasant to Speke of course. Mtesa showed distinct traits of cruelty. He thought nothing of ordering subjects off to grinding, lingering tortures and to execution; to treat them as beasts, and to countenance daily sacrifices of human beings. At times Speke's blood was roused and he dared to appeal to the monarch for clemency; nor were his desires always unheeded. With the queen-dowager, Speke was much of a favorite—she bestowed two wives upon him as a signal mark of favor, but to his disgust.

Speke's detention was a source of great annoyance to him. Through one channel only was there any prospect of release. Mtesa desired to open up his country to trade, and as Speke conversed with him repeatedly of the constant trading operations upon the Nile right

MTESA'S RESIDENCE IN UGANDA.

away north and east from Khartoum through the Soudan to the Red Sea, and of the impetus that would be given to it by extension to Uganda, if he, Speke, were permitted to go and relate all that he had seen in the kingdom, Mtesa began to think that perhaps the best course would be to allow the visitor to depart. He promised that the departure of Speke and his men should not be long delayed. This rejoiced Speke, and Grant arriving at the capital under an escort of Mtesa's men, his pleasure was unbounded.

The end came with the dawn of July 7, when Speke and Grant and their faithful henchmen bade farewell to Mtesa, bearing with them a large quantity of ivory for trade. Grant was too unwell to proceed rapidly, and it was decided that he and a portion of the caravan should march slowly to the west into Ungoro. Speke made for the head of the Victoria Lake, and on July 19, his was the magnificent reward of standing upon the banks of old Father Nile. Speke describes the scene as most beautiful. " Nothing could surpass it. It was the very perfection of the kind of effect aimed at in a highly-kept park, with a magnificent stream about 700 yards wide, dotted with islets and rocks—the former occupied by fishermen's huts, the latter by sterns and crocodiles basking in the sun—flowing between high grassy banks with rich trees and plantains in the background, where herds of hartbeests could be seen grazing, while the hippopotami were snorting in the water, and florikan and guinea-fowl, rising at our feet." A few trials more, —now in thick jungle, anon crossing streams and rapids, and among wondering and suspicious natives, and Speke was thrilled by the fact that he was standing near the head of a series of charming falls constituting the outlet

RIPON FALLS.

of the Victoria Nyanza and the principal source of old Father Nile. Here was a grand discovery indeed—one denied to all other Europeans throughout the ages in spite of unwearied searchings.

To the falls Speke gave the name of "Ripon." "Though beautiful, the scene was not exactly what I expected," Speke writes in his book, "for the broad surface of the lake was shut out from view by a spur of hill, and the falls, about twelve feet deep and 500 feet broad, were broken by rocks. Still it was a sight that attracted one to it for hours." Thence upon the bosom of the Nile, upon roughly constructed boats, Speke and his party sailed northwards for some days, to leave the water, after being attacked by Wanyoro, and to rejoin Grant, and, subsequently, the whole united caravan entered Unyoro and stood before the capital of the king, Kamrasi, who had sent the presents of fowls and plantains in token of friendship.

Like the monarch of Uganda, the king of Unyoro was surrounded by courtiers, but there was a lack of imposing ceremony. Kamrasi sat upon a stool when receiving the strangers, but there was a variety of dressed skins about and around him, and his ornaments were profuse. Speke's chronometer was a special object of envy to Kamrasi. They got on fairly well with Kamrasi, aroused his curiosity by presenting him with a Bible, spoke to him of trade, and delighted him by their prowess in the hunting-field. Hearing that the servants of Petherick, the noted English trader upon the Nile, south of Khartoum, was in the neighborhood of Gondokoro, in what has since been known as the Equatorial, or Emin's province of the Soudan, Speke and Grant were delighted beyond measure. Nearly two years had

THE SOURCES OF THE NILE. 83

elapsed since they saw a third white man, and as they were still 2000 miles from the mouth of the Nile, it may be imagined how eagerly both looked forward to the meeting.

Starting from Kamrasi's palace at last, Speke and his

A GROUP OF GANI AND MADI.

followers headed for the Nile banks, trusted themselves to the Nile waters again, passed the Karuma Falls, and through what is known as the Kidi Wilderness, and on November 29, the conical huts of the naked Koki in Gani were sighted, then the Madi, to be known hereafter by Samuel Baker, Gordon, and Emin Pasha, were seen, and the outpost of civilization, garrisoned by irregular troops in the pay of the Egyptian Government, was reached with feelings of profound gratitude, news of Petherick being a short distance away heightening the joy of the explorers. Egyptian rule as understood in the Soudan territory had become hateful and fearful to the natives, not a few of whom fled as Speke and his men advanced, not feeling safe by any means in their company. They could not know that the travelers were not plunderers. In February (1863), Gondokoro, then little more than a cluster of huts, still a trading station of some importance upon the White Nile, came in view, small sailing craft and dhows were seen, and to the unspeakable delight of Speke and Grant, Samuel Baker appeared in the midst of a throng of people to accord them the very heartiest congratulations at an escape from what he and many others believed would have been certain death in the vast lake regions. Baker had ascended the Nile thus far in search of Speke and Grant, and was prepared to go much farther. Petherick was at the moment 70 miles away, and did not come in for some time afterwards.

While Baker went exploring south-west, one result of which was the discovery of the Albert Nyanza—Speke and Grant took a voyage down the Nile to Khartoum. This took a month. On April 15, they were aboard a sailing vessel bound for Berber, whence they joined a caravan across the desert to Korosko, and took Nile boats for Cairo, where they arrived at the latter end of May, 1863. It was at Cairo that the "faithfuls" and Speke and Grant separated. The former were "paid off" and sent coastwise to their homes, *via* Zanzibar, in charge of Bombay—the two Englishmen returning to England, after an absence of four years and eight months, to be deservedly honored on every hand.

Captain Speke did not live long to enjoy his wonderful successes. He died September 15, 1864, from the effects of wounds received by him accidentally while out shooting. He was then but 38 years old.

Although not, as he supposed, the discoverer of the remotest source of the Nile, Speke was undoubtedly the first European who saw the Victoria Nyanza, while the adventurous and hazardous journey he and Grant performed together, places them in the front rank of African travelers. They opened up an extensive and rich district hitherto totally unknown, and made many important discoveries.

Captain Speke was the first to traverse the territories of those savage potentates, M'wanga, Mtesa and Kamrasi. The names of Uganda, Unyoro, the Somerset Nile, the Ripon and Karuma Falls, are now familiar in our mouths, and among the honored names of Great African Travelers, that of Speke, and in a lesser degree, of his accomplished companion, Grant, will ever hold a prominent place.

CHAPTER IX.

DAVID LIVINGSTONE.

DAVID LIVINGSTONE was born at Blantyre, near Glasgow, Scotland, about the year 1817. He worked in a cotton factory in his youth; and studied medicine and theology, with an intention to labor as a missionary, and was sent by the London Missionary Society to South Africa, in 1840. He landed at Cape Town, and for the next sixteen years of his life (to 1856) he labored in medical and missionary efforts for the good of the people, without any cost to them.

Up to this time the explorers of Africa had confined their travels to the north-western regions; they had traversed the Niger to its mouth, they had visited Timbuctoo, sailed on Lake Tchad, and crossed the continent from the Gulf of Benin to the Mediterranean. Everywhere the Europeans had passed through scenes of horror caused by the slave-hunters; ruined towns, depopulated districts, roads lined with skeletons, and caravans of negroes dragged from their homes to be sold.

From Cape Town, he went round to Algoa Bay, where he proceeded about 800 miles into the interior to Kuruman, the missionary station of the Rev. R. Moffatt, whose daughter he afterwards married.

He went on to Lepole, where he spent six months

LIVINGSTONE UNDER THE LION.

learning the language and habits of the Bakwains. These people being driven by another tribe from their country, he was unable to form a station at that place. He was more successful at Mabotsa, also inhabited by the Bakwains, to which place he removed in 1843. It was here, while chasing a lion, that he nearly lost his life. He had fired both barrels of his gun, and was reloading when the lion, though desperately wounded, sprang upon him, catching his shoulder, both man and beast coming to the ground together. Growling horribly, the fierce brute shook him as a "terrier dog does a rat." The gun of his companion missed fire, when the lion, leaving Livingstone, attacked him. Another native came up with a spear, when the lion pounced on him; but the bullets at that moment taking effect, the fierce brute fell down dead. "Besides crunching the bones into splinters, he left eleven teeth wounds upon the upper part of my arm." The wounds soon healed, but to the end of his life he occasionally felt the effects of the knawing he had received.

The chief of the Bakwains, Sechele, became a Christian, and exerted himself for the conversion of his people. The Dutch Boers (or farmers), who had pushed forward to the confines of the country, proved, however, most adverse to the success of the mission, by carrying off the natives and forcing them to labor as slaves.

By the advice of Dr. Laidley, Sechele and his people moved to the Kolobeng, a stream about 200 miles to the north of Kuruman, where Livingstone formed a station. He here built a house with his own hands, having learned carpentering and gardening from Mr. Moffatt, as also blacksmith's work. He had now become handy at almost any trade, in addition to doctoring and preaching, and as his wife could make candles, soap and clothes, they possessed what may be considered the indispensable accomplishments of a missionary family in Africa.

DAVID LIVINGSTONE.

Among the visitors to the station was Mr. Oswell, who deserves to take rank as an African traveler. Hearing that Livingstone purposed crossing the Kalahari Desert in search of the great Lake Ngami, he came from India on purpose to join him, accompanied by Mr. Murray, volunteering to pay the entire expenses of the guides.

The Kalahari, though called a desert from being composed of soft sand and being destitute of water, at this time supported prodigious herds of antelopes, while numbers of elephants, rhinoceros, lions, hyænas, and other animals roamed over it. They find support from the astonishing quantity of grass which grows in the region, as also from a species of water-melon, and tuberous roots.

Such was the desert Livingstone and his party purposed crossing when they set out with their wagons on June 1, 1849, from Kolobeng, They traversed 300 miles of desert, when at the end of a month, they reached the banks of the Zonga, a large river, richly fringed with fruit-bearing and other trees, many of them of gigantic growth, running north-east towards Lake Ngami. They were cordially received by the peace-loving inhabitants of its banks.

Leaving the wagons in charge of the natives, Livingstone embarked in one of their canoes. Frail as are the canoes of the natives, they make long trips in them, and manage them with great skill, often standing up and paddling with long, light poles. They thus daringly attack the hippopotami in their haunts, or pursue the swift antelope which ventures to swim across the river. After voyaging on the stream for twelve days, they reached the broad expanse of Lake Ngami. Though wide, it is very shallow and brackish during the rainy season. They here heard of some large rivers flowing into the lake.

Livingstone's main object in coming was to visit

Sebituane, the great chief of the Makololo, who live about 200 miles to the northward. The chief of the district refused either to give them goods or allow them to cross the river. The season being far advanced, they returned to Kolobeng, Mr. Oswell going down to the Cape to bring up a boat for the next season.

Half of the premium for the encouragement of geographical science and discoveries was awarded to Livingstone for the discoveries he made on this journey.

Sechele, the Christian chief of the Bakwains, offered his services, and with him as a guide, accompanied by Mrs. Livingstone and their three children, they set out, in April, 1850, taking a more easterly course than before.

They again reached the lake, but most of the party being attacked by fever, the design of visiting Sebituane was abandoned.

The third journey, was begun in the Spring of 1851. First traveling north, and then to the north-east, through a region covered with baobab-trees, abounding with springs, and inhabited by Bushmen, they entered an arid and difficult country. Here, the supply of water being exhausted, great anxiety was felt for the children, who suffered greatly from thirst. At length a small stream, the Mababe, was reached, running into a marsh, across which they had to make their way. During the night they traversed a region infested by the *tsetse*, a fly not much larger than the common house-fly, the bite of which destroys cattle and horses. It is remarkable that neither man, wild animals, nor even calves as long as they continue to suck, suffer from the bite of this fearful pest. While some districts are infested by it, others in the immediate neighborhood are free, and, as it does not bite at night, the only way the cattle of travelers can escape is by passing quickly through the infested district before the sun is up. Sometimes the natives lose the whole of their cattle by its attacks, and travelers frequently have been deprived of all means of moving with their wagons. Having reached the Chobe, a large river which falls into the Zambesi, leaving their attendants camped with the cattle on an island, Livingstone and his family, with Oswell, embarked in a canoe, and went down about 20 miles to an island, where Sebituane was waiting to recieve them.

The chief, pleased with the confidence Livingstone had shown in bringing his wife and children, promised to take them to see his country, that they might choose a spot to form a missionary station. He had been at war nearly all his life, with the neighboring savage tribes, but had got himself in a secure position behind the Chobe and Leeambye, whose broad streams guarded him from the inroads of his enemies. He had more subjects and was richer in cattle than any chief in that part of Africa. The rivers and swamps, however, of the region produced fever, which proved fatal to many of his people. He was anxious for intercourse with Europeans, and showed every wish to encourage those who now visited him to remain in his territory. A few days later the chief was attacked with inflammation of the lungs, and in a short time breathed his last. Before his death he expressed the hope that the English would be as friendly to his children as they had been to himself. The chieftainship devolved on a daughter, who gave the visitors leave to travel through any part of the country they chose. They accordingly set out, and traversing 130 miles to the north-east, reached the banks of the Zambesi, the chief river of Southern Africa.

From the prevalence of the *tsetse*, and the periodical rise of the numerous streams causing malaria, Livingstone was compelled to abandon the intention he had formed of removing the Bakwain people thither that

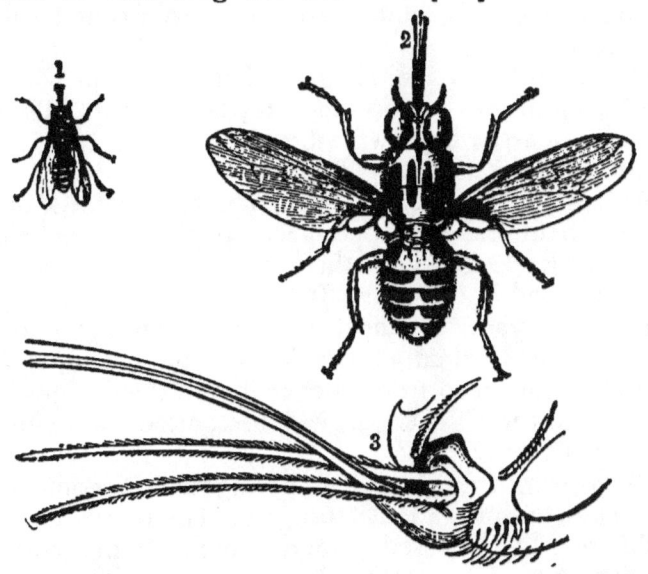

1. THE TSETSE. 2. THE SAME MAGNIFIED. 3. THE PROBOSCIS.

they might be out of the reach of their rapacious neighbors, the Dutch Boers. The river was, he at once saw, the key of Southern Africa. This was a most important discovery, for that river was not previously known to exist there.

The magnificent stream, on the bank of which he now stood, flows hundreds of miles east to the Indian Ocean

—a mighty artery supplying life to the teeming population of that part of Africa.

Livingstone determined to send his wife and children to England, and to return himself and spend two or three years in the new region he had discovered, in the hopes of evangelizing the people and putting a stop to the trade in slaves, which had begun even thus far from the coast.

He returned to Kolobeng, and then set out with his family, a journey of 1000 miles, to Cape Town. Placing them on board a homeward-bound ship, he turned his face northward in June, 1852.

As Livingstone's chief object was to select a spot for a settlement, he ascended, accompanied by Sekeletu, the great River Zambesi, the upper courses of which he had traversed in the year 1851.

From Linyanti Livingstone set out on his journey westward to Loanda, on the West Coast, and, on his return, commenced from thence that adventurous expedition to the East Coast, which resulted in so many important discoveries.

Recovering from his fever, Livingstone, accompanied by Sekeletu and about 160 attendants, set out for Sesheke. They passed numerous mounds, the work of *termites* or white ants; which are literally gigantic structures, and often wild date-trees were seen growing on them.

Livingstone had a little gipsy tent in which he slept, though the Makololo huts, which are kept tolerably clean, afforded the party accommodation. The best sort of hut consists of three circular walls, having small holes to serve as doors, through which it is necessary to creep on all fours. The roof resembles in shape a

Chinaman's hat, and is bound together with circular bands. The framework is first formed, and it is then

HOUSE-BUILDING.

lifted to the top of the circle of poles prepared for supporting it.

The roof is covered with fine grass and sewed with

the same material as the lashings. Women are the chief builders of huts among the Makololo.

Reaching the village of Katonga, on the banks of the Leeambye, some time was spent there in collecting canoes. During this delay Dr. Livingstone visited the country to the north of the village, where he saw large herds of buffaloes, zebras, and elans. He was enabled, by this hunting expedition, to supply his companions with an abundance of food.

A sufficient number of canoes being collected, they began the ascent of the river. Livingstone's canoe had six paddlers, while Sekeletu's had ten. The men paddled standing upright, and kept stroke with great exactness. Being flat-bottomed, they can float in very shallow water. The fleet consisted altogether of 33 canoes and 160 men.

During this nine weeks' tour Livingstone took a more intense disgust of heathenism than he had ever before felt, and formed a higher opinion of the civilizing effects of the missions in the south among tribes which were once as savage as the Makololo.

Returning down the stream at a rapid rate, they quickly reached Linyanti.

The chief agreeing that the object of Livingstone's expedition to the west was desirable, took pains to assist him. A band of 27 men were to accompany him by the chief's command, whose desire was to obtain a free and profitable trade with the white men, and this, Livingstone was convinced, would lead to their elevation and improvement.

As they approached the sea, the Makololo gazed at it, spreading out before them, with feelings of awe, having before believed that the whole world was one

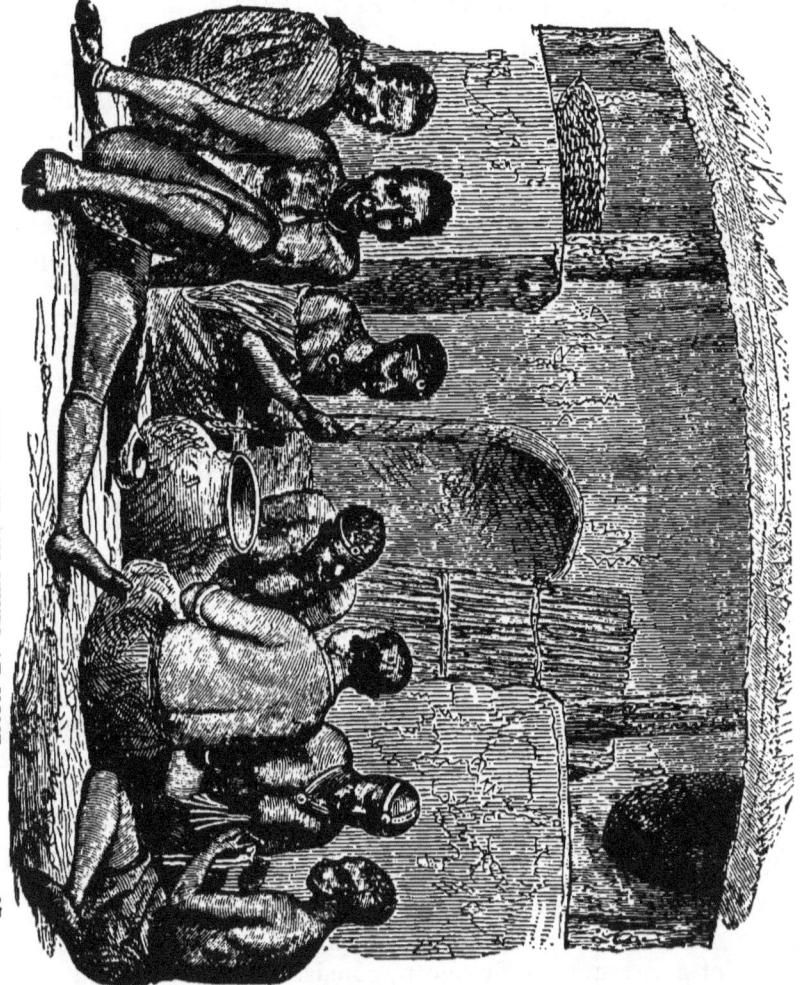

A MAKOLOLO CHIEF AND HIS WIVES AT HOME.

extended plain. They again showed their fears that they might be kidnapped, but Livingstone reassured them, telling them as they had stood by each other hitherto, so they would do to the last.

On May 31, they descended a declivity leading to the city of Loanda, where Livingstone was warmly welcomed by Mr. Gabriel, the British commissioner for the suppression of the slave trade. Seeing him so ill, he offered his bed to him. "Never shall I forget," says Livingstone, "the luxurious pleasure I enjoyed in feeling myself again on a good couch, after for six months sleeping on the ground."

It took many days before he recovered, from the exposure and fatigue he had endured. All that time he was watched over with the most generous sympathy by his kind host.

His men, while he was unable to attend to them, employed themselves in going into the country and cutting firewood, which they sold to the inhabitants of the town. Mr. Gabriel also found them employment in unloading a collier, at sixpence a day. They continued at this work for upwards of a month, astonished at the vast amount of "stones that burn" which were taken out of her. With the money they purchased clothing, beads and other articles to carry home with them.

From the kind and generous treatment Livingstone received from the Portuguese, they rose deservedly high in his estimation.

He now prepared for his departure. The merchants sent a present to Sekeletu, consisting of specimens of all their articles of trade and two donkeys, that the breed might be introduced into his country, as the *tsetse* cannot kill those beasts. Livingstone was furnished with letters of recommendation to the Portuguese authorities in Eastern Africa.

They were now accompanied by their Portuguese friends, the Londa people, who inhabit the banks of the Loajima.

They elaborately dress their hair in a number of ways. It naturally hangs down on their shoulders in large masses, which, with their general features, gives them a strong resemblance to the ancient Egyptians.

MEN'S HEAD-DRESSES.

Some of them twist their hair into a number of small cords, which they stretch out to a hoop encircling the head. Others adorn their heads with ornaments of woven hair and hide, to which they suspend the tails of buffaloes. Some weave the hair on pieces of hide in the form of buffalo horns, projecting on either side of the head. The young men twine their hair in the form of a single horn, projecting over their forehead in front. They frequently tattoo their bodies, producing figures in the form of stars. Although their heads are thus elaborately adorned, their bodies are almost naked.

Reaching Calongo, Livingstone directed his course towards the territory of his old friend, Katema; which they reached on June 2.

They now took their way across the level plain, which had been flooded on their former journey. Vultures were flying in the air, showing the quantity of carrion which had been left by the waters.

They passed Lake Dilolo, a sheet of water six or eight miles long and two broad. The sight of the blue waters had a soothing effect on Livingstone, who was suffering from fever, after his journey through the gloomy forest and across the wide flat.

Old Shinti, whose capital they now reached, received them in a friendly way, and supplied them with provisions. They left with him a number of plants, among which were orange, cashew, custard, apple, and fig-trees, with coffee, acacias, and papaws, which he had brought from Loanda. They were planted out in the enclosure of one of his principal men, with a promise that Shinti should have a share of them when grown.

They now again embarked in six small canoes on the waters of the Leeba. Paddling down it, they next entered the Leeambye. Here they found a party of hunt-

VICTORIA FALLS, ZAMBESI RIVER.

ers, who had been engaged in stalking buffaloes, hippopotami, and other animals.

On reaching the town of Lebouta they were welcomed with joy, the women coming out, dancing and singing, Livingstone now heard that the trading party which set out, reached Loanda in safety, and it must have been a great satisfaction to him to feel that he had thus opened out a way to the enterprise of these industrious and intelligent people.

The donkeys which had been brought excited much admiration, and, as they were not affected by the bite of the *tsetse*, it was hoped that they might prove of great use. Their music, however, startled the inhabitants more than the roar of lions.

Arrangements were now made for performing another adventurous journey to the East Coast.

As soon as Livingstone announced his intention of proceeding to the east, numerous volunteers came forward to accompany him. From among them he selected 114 trustworthy men. They sailed down the river to its confluence with the Chobe; reaching this spot, they prepared to strike across country to the northeast, in order to reach the northern bank of the Zambesi. Before doing so, Livingstone determined to visit the Victoria Falls, of which he had often heard. The meaning of the word is: "Smoke does sound there," in reference to the vapor and noise produced by the falls. After twenty minutes' sail from Kalai, they came in sight of five columns of vapor, appropriately called "smoke," rising at a distance of five or six miles off, and bending as they ascended before the wind, the tops appearing to mingle with the clouds. The scene was beautiful. The banks and the islands which appeared

CURIOUS MODE OF SALUTATION.

here and there amid the stream, were richly adorned with trees and shrubs of various colors, many being in full blossom. High above all rose an enormous baobab-tree, surrounded by groups of graceful palms.

As the water was now low, they proceeded in the canoe to an island in the centre of the river, the further end of which extended to the edge of the falls. At the spot where they landed it was impossible to discover where the vast body of water disappeared. It seemed suddenly to sink into the earth, for the opposite lip of the fissure into which it descends was only eighty feet distant. On peering over the precipice the doctor saw the stream, 1000 yards broad, leaping down 100 feet and then becoming suddenly compressed into a space of 20 yards, when, instead of flowing as before, it turned directly to the right, and went boiling and rushing amid the hills.

The vapor which rushes up from this caldron to the height of 300 feet, being condensed, changes its hue to that of dark smoke, and then comes down in a constant shower. The chief portion falls on the opposite side of the fissure, where grow a number of evergreen trees, their leaves always wet. The walls of this gigantic crack are perpendicular. Livingstone considered these falls the most wonderful sight he had beheld.

Returning to Kalai, the party met Sekeletu, and, bidding him a final farewell, set off northwards to Lekone, through a beautiful country, on November 20. The farther they advanced the more the country swarmed with inhabitants, and great numbers came to see the white men, invariably bringing presents of maize.

The natives of this region have a curious way of

saluting a stranger. Instead of bowing they throw themselves on their backs on the ground, rolling from side to side and slapping the outsides of their thighs, while they utter the words, "*Kina bomba! kina bomba!*" In vain Livingstone implored them to stop. They, imagining him pleased, only tumbled about more fiercely and slapped their thighs with greater vehemence. These villagers supplied the party with ground-nuts, maize and corn.

The inhabitants of the north side of the Zambesi are the Batonga; those on the south bank, the Banyai.

At each village they passed, two men were supplied to conduct them to the next, and lead them through the parts least covered with jungle.

The villagers were busily employed in their gardens. Most of the men have muscular figures. Their color varies from a dark to a light olive. The women have the extraordinary custom of piercing the upper lip, and gradually enlarging the orifice till a ring can be inserted. The lip appears drawn out beyond the nose, and gives them a very ugly appearance. As Sekwebu remarked: "These women want to make their mouths like those of ducks." The commonest of these rings are made of bamboo, but others are made of ivory or metal.

The favorite weapon of the Banyai is a huge axe, which is carried over the shoulder. It is used chiefly for hamstringing the elephant.

Those curious birds, the "honey guides," were very attentive to them, and, by their means, the Makololo obtained an abundance of honey. Of the wax, however, in those districts no use appears to be made.

It was not till March 20 that Tete was reached. Livingstone was then so prostrated that, though only eight miles from it, he could proceed no farther. He forwarded the letters of recommendation he received in Angola to the commandant. The following morning a company of soldiers with an officer arrived, bringing the materials for a civilized breakfast, and a litter in which to carry him. He felt so greatly revived by the breakfast that he was able to walk the whole way.

Tete is a mere village, built on a slope reaching to the water, close to which the fort is situated. There are about thirty European houses; the rest of the buildings, inhabited by the natives, are of wattle and daub.

Formerly, besides gold-dust and ivory, large quantities of grain, coffee, sugar, oil and indigo were exported from Tete, but, on the establishment of the slave-trade, the merchants found a more speedy way of becoming rich by selling off their slaves, and the plantations and gold-washings were abandoned, the laborers having been exported to the Brazils. Many of the white men then followed their slaves. After this, a native of Goa, Nyaude by name, built a stockade at the confluence of the Luenya and Zambesi, took the commandant of Tete, who attacked him, prisoner, and sent his son Bonga with a force against that town and burned it. Others followed his example, till commerce, before rendered stagnant by the slave-trade, was totally obstructed.

The forests in the neighborhood abound with elephants, and the natives attack them in the boldest manner. Only two hunters sally forth together—one carrying spears, the other an axe of a peculiar shape, with a long handle. As soon as an elephant is discovered, the man with the spears creeps among the bushes in front of it, so as to attract its attention, during which time the axe-man

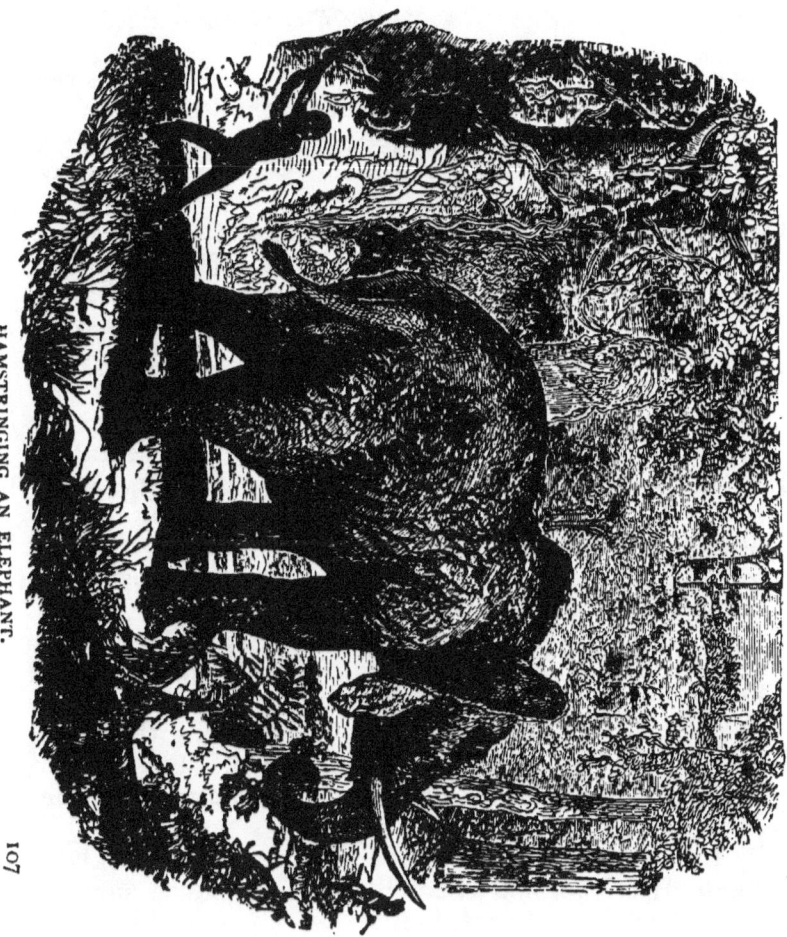
HAMSTRINGING AN ELEPHANT.

cautiously approaches from behind, and with a sweep of his formidable weapon, severs the tendon of the animal's hock. The huge creature, now unable to move, in spite of its strength and sagacity falls an easy prey to the two hunters.

Among other valuable productions of the country is found a tree allied to the cinchona. The Portuguese believe that it has the same virtues as quinine.

After waiting about six weeks at Quillimane, an English brig arrived, on board of which Livingstone embarked.

Having been three and a half years, with the exception of a short interval in Angola, without speaking English, and for thirteen but partially using it, Livingstone found the greatest difficulty in expressing himself on board the ship.

The brig sailed on July 12, for the Mauritius, which was reached on August 12.

After remaining some time at the Mauritius, till he had recovered from the effects of the African fever, our enterprising traveler sailed by way of the Red Sea for England, which he reached on December 12, 1856, after an absence of 16 years; during which time he had traversed 11,000 miles, and crossed the continent from west to east.

Livingstone, in the series of journeys which have been described, had accomplished more than any previous traveler in Africa, besides having gained information of the greatest value as regards both missionary and mercantile enterprise. He had as yet, however, performed only a portion of the great work his untiring zeal and energy had prompted him to undertake.

CHAPTER X.

Dr. Livingstone's Second Expedition to Explore the Zambesi.

LIVINGSTONE passed more than a year in England, and on March 10, 1858, sailed in the *Pearl*, at the head of a Government expedition for the purpose of exploring the Zambesi and the neighboring region. He was accompanied by Dr. Kirk, his brother, Charles Livingstone, and Mr. Thornton; and Mr. Baines was appointed artist to the expedition.

A small steamer, which was called the *Ma-Robert*, in compliment to Mrs. Livingstone, was provided by the Government for the navigation of the river.

The East Coast was reached in May. Running up the River Luawe, supposed to be a branch of the Zambesi, the *Pearl* came to anchor, and the *Ma-Robert*, which had been brought out in sections, was screwed together. The two vessels then went together in search of the true mouth of the river from which Quillimane is some 60 miles distant, the Portuguese having concealed the real entrance, in order to deceive the English cruisers in search of slavers. The crew consisted of about a dozen Krumen and a few Europeans.

On August 17, 1858, the *Ma-Robert* began her voyage

up the stream for Tete. It was soon found that from her furnaces being badly constructed, she was ill adapted for the work before her. She soon obtained the name of the *Asthmatical.*

Tete was reached on September 8. No sooner did Livingstone go on shore, than his Makololo rushed down to the water's edge and manifested the greatest joy at seeing him. The Portuguese at this place keep slaves, whom they treat with tolerable humanity. When they can, they purchase the whole of a family, thus taking away the chief inducement for running off.

The expedition, hearing of the Kebrabasa Falls, steamed up the river, and on November 14, reached Panda Mokua, where the navigation ends, about two miles below them. Hence the party started overland, by a frightfully rough path among rocky hills, where no shade was to be found. At last their guides declared that they could go no farther; indeed, the surface of the ground was so hot that the soles of the Makololo's feet became blistered. The travelers, however, pushed on. Passing round a steep promontory, they beheld the river at their feet, the channel jammed in between two mountains with perpendicular sides, and less than fifty yards wide. When the river rises upwards of 80 feet, as it does in the rainy season, the cataract might be passed in boats.

After returning to Tete, the steamer went up the Shiré, January, 1859. The natives, as they passed them, collected at their villages in large numbers, armed with bows and poisoned arrows, threatening to attack them. Livingstone went on shore, and explained to the chief, that they had come neither to take slaves nor to fight, but wished to open up a path by which his countrymen

KRUMEN AND THEIR CANOES.

could ascend to purchase their cotton. On this the chief became friendly.

Their progress was arrested, after steaming up 100 miles in a straight line (although, counting the windings of the river, double that distance), by magnificent cataracts, to which Livingstone gave the name of the Murchison Falls, after the President of the Geographical Society.

Rain prevented them making observations, and they returned at a rapid rate down the river. A second trip up the Shiré was made in March.

They returned to Tete on June 23, 1859, and thence proceeded to the Kongone, where they received provisions from the *Persian*, which also took on board their Krumen, as they were found useless for land journeys. In their stead a crew was picked out from the Makololo, who soon learned to work the ship, and who, besides being good travelers, could cut wood and required only native food. Frequent showers fell on their return voyage up the Zambesi, and the vessel being leaky, the cabin was constantly flooded.

A second trip up the Shiré was performed in the middle of August, when they set out in search of Lake Nyassa, about which they had heard. The river, though narrow, is deeper than the Zambesi, and more easily navigated. On both banks a number of hippopotamus traps were seen.

The animal feeds on grass alone, its enormous lip acting like a mowing machine, forming a path before it as it feeds. Over these paths the natives construct a trap, consisting of a heavy beam, five or six feet long, with a spear head at one end, covered with poison. This weapon is hung to a forked pole by a rope which

SPEARING THE HIPPOPOTAMUS.

leads across the path, and is held by a catch, set free as the animal treads upon it. A hippopotamus was seen which, being frightened by the steamer, rushed on shore and ran immediately under one of these traps, when down came the heavy beam on its head.

On August 28, 1859, an expedition, consisting of four whites, 36 Makololo, and two guides, left the ship in the hope of discovering Lake Nyassa. The natives on the road were eager to trade. As soon as they found that the strangers would pay for their provisions in cotton cloth, women and girls were sent to grind and pound meal, and the men and boys were seen chasing screaming fowl over the village.

The Highland women of these regions all wear the lip-ring. An old chief, when asked why such things were worn, replied: "For beauty; men have beards and whiskers, women have none. What kind of a creature would a woman be with whiskers and without the ring?"

When, as they calculated, they were about a day's march from Lake Nyassa, the chief of the village assured them that no lake had ever been heard of there, and that the River Shiré stretched on, as they saw it, to a distance of two months, and then came out between two rocks which towered to the skies. The Makololo looked blank and proposed returning to the ship.

"Never mind," said Livingstone, "we will go on and see these wonderful rocks."

Their head man, Massakasa, declared that there must be a lake, because it was in the white men's books, and scolded the natives for speaking a falsehood. They then admitted that there was a lake.

The expedition moving forward, on September 16,

1859. The long-looked-for Lake Nyassa was discovered, with hills rising on both sides.

Dr. Kirk and Mr. Rae, the engineer, set off with guides to go across the country to Tete, the distance

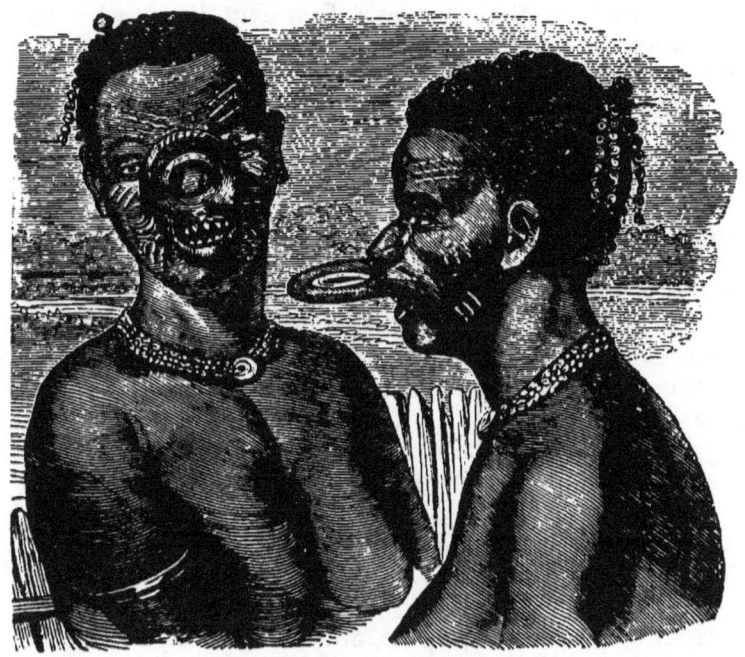

PELELE, OR LIP-RING.

being about 100 miles. From want of water they suffered greatly, while the *tsetse* infested the district.

Livingstone returned in the *Ma-Robert* once more to the Kongone. After this trip, the poor *Asthmatical* broke down completely.

Active preparations were now made for the intended journey westward; cloth, beads and brass wire were formed into packages, with the bearer's name printed on each.

The Makololo who had been employed by the expedition received their wages. Some of those who had remained at Tete had married, and resolved to continue where they were.

All arrangements had been concluded by May 15, 1860, and the journey was begun. On August 4, the expedition reached Moachemba, the first of the Batoka villages which owe allegiance to Sekeletu. From thence, beyond a beautiful valley, the columns of vapor rising from the Victoria Falls, upwards of 20 miles away, could clearly be distinguished.

The travelers landed at the head of Garden Island, and, Livingstone peered over the giddy heights at the farther end across the chasm. The measurement of the chasm was now taken; it was found to be 80 yards opposite Garden Island, while the waterfall itself was twice the depth of that of Niagara, and the river where it went over the rock fully a mile wide. Charles Livingstone, who had seen Niagara, pronounced it inferior in magnificence to the Victoria Falls.

The Batokas consider Garden Island and another farther west as sacred spots, and here, in days gone by, they assembled to worship the Deity.

Zumbo was reached on November 1, 1860, and Tete on the 23d, the expedition having been absent rather more than six months. They were glad to find that the two English sailors were in good health, and had behaved very well; but their farm had been a failure. One night a hippopotamus destroyed their vegetable garden, the sheep ate up their cotton plants, while the crocodiles carried off the sheep, and the natives had stolen their fowls.

On December 31, the *Pioneer*, the steamer which had been sent to replace the *Asthmatical*, appeared off the bar, but the bad weather prevented her entering. At the same time two men-of-war arrived, bringing Bishop Mackenzie, at the head of the Oxford and Cambridge mission to the tribes of the Shiré and Lake Nyassa. It consisted of six Englishmen and five colored men from the Cape.

Charles Livingstone collected specimens of cotton, and upwards of 300 pounds were obtained, at a price of a penny a pound, which showed that cotton of a superior quality could be raised by native labor alone and that but for the slave-trade a large amount might be raised in the country.

Wherever they went they gained the confidence of the people, and hitherto the expedition had been very successful. No sooner did they come in contact with the Portuguese slave-trade than reverses commenced. Plundering parties of the Ajawa were desolating the land, and a gang had crossed the river with slaves.

They halted at the village of their old friend, Mpende, who supplied them with carriers and informed them that a slave party, on its way to Tete, would soon pass through his village. Soon afterwards this party, consisting of a long line of manacled men, women and children, escorted by black drivers, armed with muskets, adorned with articles of finery, and blowing horns, marched by them with a triumphant air. As soon as the rascals caught sight of the English, they darted off into the forest, with the exception of the leader, who was seized by the Makololo. He proved to be a slave of the late commandant of Tete, and was well known to them. He declared that he had bought the slaves; but directly his hands were released he bolted.

The captives, now kneeling down, expressed their thanks by clapping their hands. Knives were soon busily at work setting free the women and children. It was more difficult to liberate the men, who had each his neck in the fork of a stout stick, six or seven feet long, and kept in by an iron rod riveted at both ends across the throat. A saw did the work. The men could scarcely believe what was said, when they were told to take the meal they were carrying and cook breakfast for themselves and children. Many of the latter were about five years of age and under. One of them observed to the men: "Those others tied and starved us, you cut the ropes, and tell us to eat. What sort of people are you?"

Eighty-four persons, chiefly women and children, were thus liberated; and being told that they might go where they liked, they decided on remaining with the English.

Eight others were freed in a hamlet on the road; but another party, with nearly 100 slaves, though followed by Dr. Kirk and his four Makololo, escaped. Six more captives were soon afterwards liberated, and two slave-dealers were detained for the night, but being carelessly watched, they escaped. The next day 50 more slaves were freed at another village and comfortably clothed.

Marching forward, on January 22, 1861, news was received that the Ajawa were near, burning villages and killing the people.

It was evident that the Ajawa was instigated by the

MURCHISON FALLS.

Portuguese agents from Tete. It was possible that they might by persuasion be induced to follow the better course, but, from their long habit of slaving for the Quillimane market, this appeared doubtful. The Bishop consulted Livingstone as to whether, should his assistance be asked against the Ajawà, it would be his duty to give it? He displayed his usual sagacity in his reply: "Do not interfere in native quarrels."

Leaving the members of the mission camped on a beautiful spot, near the clear little stream of Magomero, the expedition returned to the ship to prepare for their journey to Lake Nyassa.

On August 6, 1861, Livingstone, Kirk and Charles Livingstone started in a four-oared gig, with one white sailor and 20 Makololo for Nyassa. Carriers were easily engaged to convey the boat past the 40 miles of the Murchison Cataracts. Several volunteers came forward, and the men of one village transported it to the next. They passed the little Lake of Pamalombe, about ten miles long and five broad, surrounded thickly by papyrus. Myriads of mosquitos showed the presence of malaria, and they hastened past it.

Again launching their boat, they proceeded up the river, and entered the lake on September 2 1861, greatly refreshed by the cool air which came off its wide expanse of water. The centre appeared to be of a deep blue, while the shallow water along the edge was indicated by its light green color. A little distance from the shore the water was 75 feet in depth, but round a grand mountain promontory no bottom could be obtained with their lead-line of over 200 feet. Lake Nyassa was estimated to be about 200 miles long, and from twenty to sixty broad, and appeared to be surrounded by moun-

ZULUS.

tains, but on the west they were merely the edges of a high table-land.

Nyassa is visited by sudden and tremendous storms. Every night they hauled the boat up on the beach; and, had it not been supposed that these storms were peculiar to one season, they would have given the Nyassa the name of the "Lake of Storms."

A dense population exists on the shores of the lake, including a tribe of Zulus who came from the south some years ago. The people cultivate the soil, growing large quantities of rice, sweet potatoes, maize and millet. Those at the north end reap a curious harvest. Clouds of what appeared to be smoke rising from miles of burning grass were seen in the distance. The appearance was caused by countless millions of midges, called "kungo" by the natives. As the boat passed through them, eyes and mouth had to be kept closed. The people collect these insects by night, and boil them into thick cakes, to be eaten as a relish.

Abundance of fish were caught, some with nets and others with hook and line. Women were seen fishing, with babies on their backs. Enormous crocodiles were seen, but, as they can obtain abundance of fish, they seldom attack men.

The lake tribes appear to be open-handed, and, whenever a net was drawn, fish was always offered. On one occasion the inhabitants, on their arrival, took out their seine, dragged it, and made their visitors a present of the entire haul. The chief treated them with great kindness.

On the high lands at the northern end, a tribe of Zulus, known as the Mazitu, make sudden swoops on the hamlets of the plains, and carry off the inhabitants and burn villages.

ZANZIBAR.

The slave-trade on the lake was pursued with fearful activity. A dhow had been built by two Arabs, who were running her regularly, crowded with slaves, across its waters. Part of the captives were carried to the Portuguese slave-exporting town of Iboe, while others were sent to Kilwa.

The chiefs showed but little inclination to trade, their traffic being chiefly in human chattels. The Consul at Zanzibar, stated that 19,000 slaves, from the Nyassa country alone, passed at this time annually through the custom-house at Zanzibar.

They, however, represent but a small portion of the sufferers. Besides those actually captured, thousands were killed and died of their wounds and famine, and thousands more perished in internecine war waged for slaves with their own clansmen and neighbors. The numerous skeletons seen among rocks and woods, by the pools, and on the paths of the wilderness, attested the awful sacrifice of human life.

Livingstone saw that a small armed steamer on Lake Nyassa could, by furnishing goods in exchange for ivory and other products, exercise a powerful influence in stopping the traffic in that quarter.

The expedition had spent from September 2 to October 27 in exploring the lake, and their goods being now expended, it was found necessary to return to the ship. The Zambesi was reached on January 11, 1862.

On January 30, 1862, the *Gorgon* arrived, towing the brig which brought out Mrs. Livingstone and some ladies about to join the University mission, as well as the sections of a new iron steamer intended for the navigation of Lake Nyassa. The name of *Lady Nyassa* was given to the new vessel. Mrs. Livingstone was attacked by fever, and died on April 27, 1862.

Hoping that the *Lady Nyassa* might be the means of putting a check on the slavers across the lake, they hurried on with their work. She was unscrewed below the first cataract, and they began to make a road over the *portage* of 40 miles, by which she was to be carried piecemeal.

Trees had to be cut down and stones removed. The first half-mile of road was formed up a gradual slope till 200 feet above the river was reached, where a sensible difference in the climate was felt. Before much progress was made, Dr. Kirk and Charles Livingstone were seized with fever, and it was deemed necessary to send them home. Soon afterwards Livingstone was himself attacked.

On June 16, the remaining members started for the upper cataracts. Cotton of superior quality was seen dropping off the bushes, with no one to gather it. The huts in several villages were found entire, with mortars and stones for pounding and grinding corn, empty corn safes and kitchen utensils, water and beer pots untouched, but the doors were shut, as if the inhabitants had gone to search for roots or fruit and had never returned; while in others, skeletons were seen of persons who died apparently while endeavoring to reach something to allay the gnawings of hunger.

Several journeys had been made over the *portage*, when, on returning to the ship on July 2, they received a despatch from England, directing the return home of the expedition.

Considering the utter devastation caused by the slave-hunting, and the secret support given by the Portuguese officials to the slave-traders, notwithstanding the protestations of their government that they wished to put an end to the trade, it was impossible not to agree in the wisdom of this determination.

Altogether in this expedition they traveled 760 miles in a straight line, averaging about 15 miles a day, and they reached the ship on November 1, 1862, where all were found in good health and spirits.

Soured and disappointed at the non-success of the expedition, Livingstone now returned to England, where he arrived on July 20, 1864.

CHAPTER XI.

Travels of Sir Samuel and Lady Baker.

Samuel Baker came to his majority with a fair education, a liberal inheritance, which relieved him from any claims of business, and an engrossing spirit of adventure.

He was known as an experienced traveler and practised sportsman in Ceylon, when, in March, 1861, having resolved to devote his energies to the discovery of the sources of the Nile, and the exploration of Central Africa, he set forth from England to trace the mysterious river from its mouth. He was accompanied by his young wife, who, notwithstanding the dangers and difficulties she knew must be enconntered, entreated permission to be the companion of his travels.

The geography of Equatorial Africa had already been attacked from several quarters. The problem of the Niger had been solved. The traditions concerning a vast interior lake had been more than verified, as two great lakes had been determined. Speke and Grant were already prosecuting the journey which would demonstrate the Victoria Nyanza to be the reservoir of the White Nile; while Livingstone was at work upon the territory farther south and east. The Blue Nile was known; that the White Nile was the outlet of the

Victoria Nyanza was an accepted theory rather than a demonstrated fact, the objective of expeditions already afield. The sources of the western tributaries of the great river has not yet been determined, and to these points Baker addressed himself.

His first essay was an exploration of territory already fairly known, where he carefully mapped the Nile tributaries of Abyssinia, and served his apprenticeship for severer labors. In the last month of 1862 he left Khartoum for an exploration of the upper Nile. After two months he met Speke and Grant, who were tracing northward the outlet of the Nyanza, and so much of the determination was completed. Pushing his own expedition still farther to the southward, he broke into new territory, which he traversed under great difficulties, until after the toil of a year he was rewarded by the discovery of the Albert Nyanza, then believed to be second of the great Nile reservoirs. The subsequent discovery by Stanley of the Albert Edward Nyanza, a smaller body of water at a greater elevation, whose waters flow through the Albert Lake, has recognized in the more elevated lake the second source of the Nile. With the finding of the Albert Nyanza, Baker's labors as a discoverer were substantially closed.

The second great enterprise undertaken by Baker was at the instance of Ismail Pasha, the Khedive of Egypt, and with the authority of the Egyptian Government; it was the herculean task of suppressing the slave-trade within the jurisdiction of Egypt.

The year 1869 saw the inauguration of the Suez Canal, and the high tide of apparent Egyptian prosperity. The eyes of the world were upon the rejuvenated kingdom of the Pharaohs. The Khedive, dazzled by the achievement, aspired to be an independent ruler, to obtain possession of all the territory tributary to the Nile, and to acquire a place in the charmed circle of European rulers. He leaned upon the strong arm of England; and to secure the sympathy of that mighty power, he proposed to destroy the trade in slaves in all his realm.

SAMUEL AND LADY BAKER.

As a step toward the accomplishment of these purposes, in May, 1869, he issued a firman in which he proposed to subdue the countries about the great Equatorial lakes, to suppress the slave-trade, and to introduce a system of commerce and the navigation of the lakes. The enterprise was entrusted to Baker for four years; he was made a Pasha, given the rank of major-general, and was clothed with supreme and absolute power, including that of death, over all connected with his expedition.

Like every other scheme for real progress, proposed by Egyptian or Turk, the only validity of these propositions lay in their paper announcements. Men and materials were wanting either in quantity or quality suited to the enterprise. The real question was how not to do it. The slave-trade was to be suppressed, but the slave-trader, and his powerful and subsidized friends at court, were not to be hurt. The land was a land of paradox, and the labor was the task of Sisyphus.

With such means as he could get, Baker moved to the scene of operations. He occupied Gondokoro, the farthest important point towards the south, and made it his capital and base of operations, with the new name Ismalia. He made friends with some of the chiefs in the country beyond; others he coerced into a pretence of friendship. Then he fought his way southward, and after a continuous and harrassing campaign he placed under subjection the whole territory assigned as a theatre to his operations. By then the period named in his commission had expired, and he returned to Cairo, where he transferred his command to one whom he himself had named as his successor, that remarkable figure in modern English history, Colonel Gordon, of Chinese and afterward of Egyptian fame.

In the four years of Baker's administration of the Equatorial provinces he had accomplished scarcely more than to lay the foundation of Egyptian authority, with the subjection of the native tribes. Commerce, except the united movement of ivory and slaves, could follow only a more advanced civilization. The slave-trade

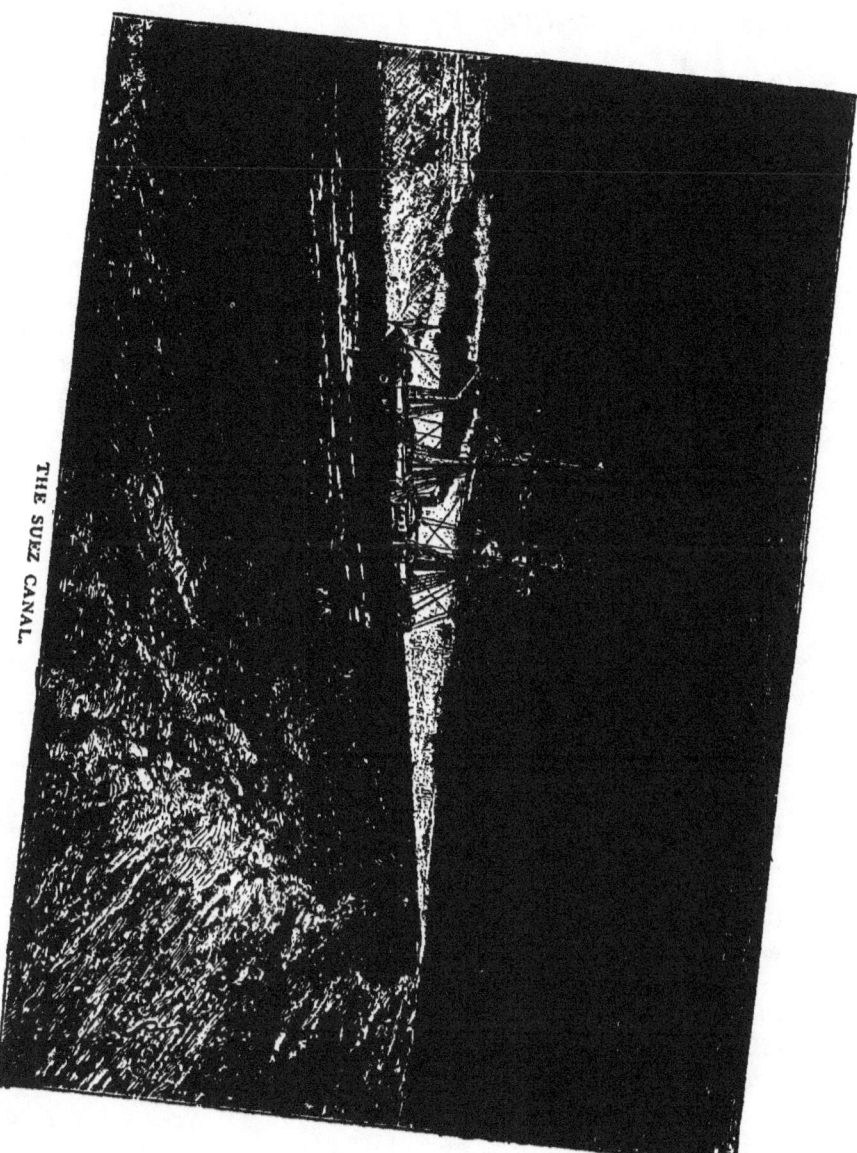

THE SUEZ CANAL.

was a disease of the social system, as fixed and as fatal as the leprosy which has once fastened its fangs upon the human frame. None of the objectives assigned to his enterprise could be established in the brief period of four years, even under favorable auspices. Could his strong hand and vigorous intellect have ruled during a period of longer duration, the result would have been more nearly commensurate with the effort.

Baker's commission expired in 1873; Gordon's followed in 1875, and lasted until 1879. During that period, great changes occurred in Egypt. The golden era of Ismail passed, and Tewfik followed his deposed father. War pitted the Russian against the Turk. England came to the succor of the "sick man," taking Cyprus for a doctor's fee, and postponing all dreams of Egyptian independence. To secure the debts incurred by Ismail's extravagance, Egypt passed under the dual control of the English and French; Arabi revolted; the bombardment of Alexandria was followed by the campaign in the desert, and the victory at Tel-el-Kebir. The fanaticism of the Moslem and the Bedouin was aroused, and an insurrection under the leadership of a self-styled prophet, the Mahdi, spread like a pestilence until it had involved the whole of Soudan and of the Equatorial provinces which Baker and Gordon had so laboriously subjugated.

In 1884 Gordon was sent back to Khartoum as one whose person and prestige could repeat in the Soudan what they had effected in China. Neglected by Egypt and abandoned by England, in 1885 he sealed with his life a devotion which was ill-compensated by the bronze effigy quickly placed in St. Paul's to typify a nation's contrition.

GONDOROKO, OR ISMALIA.

Baker had cause to feel bitterly the conduct of the English Government in the reversal of the policy of the Khedive in administering as an Egyptian satrapy the vast territories in Central Africa, of which the annexation of the Equatorial Province was his handiwork. He had cause to approve Gordon's saying, " We are a wonderful people. It was never the Government that made us a great nation. It has always been the drag upon our wheels."

On Emin Pasha taking service with the German Government in their East African possessions in 1890, after his rescue by Stanley, Baker wrote as follows on the situation at the time he and Gordon relinquished the government of the Equatorial Province, and as it had become under the new order of affairs: —

" From 1869 until General Gordon quitted the Soudan we built up a grand fabric of British influence, and linked the Albert Nyanza in direct steam communication with Khartoum. The British Government did not see it, although the slave-trade of the White Nile was suppressed, and a good government was established throughout the basin of the Nile, with far greater content to the governed than we can boast in Ireland.

" England knocked all this progressive influence on the head. All that Englishmen had achieved, first in independent exploration of the Nile sources by Speke and Grant, from the south, by myself from the north; subsequently Ismail's expedition under my own command to annex the Equatorial regions and suppress the slave-trade; then—after nearly five years by the late General Gordon's untiring energy in consolidating and extending the work which I had commenced—all had been paralyzed by England.

BAKER'S DEPARTURE FROM KHARTOUM.

"Fifteen steamers were plying up the Blue and the White Niles, and two upon the Albert Nyanza.

"The produce of the Equatorial regions, which, excepting ivory, could not bear the ordinary cost of transport, could be delivered at Khartoum by the bi-monthly steamers from Gondokoro, as, being Government vessels, they might as well travel full as empty, without additional expense.

"All this wonderful progress had been achieved within the extraordinary interval of 20 years, before which the sources of the Nile were as dark a mystery as they had been 5000 years ago. The British Government had no hand in this; the instruments were individual Englishmen. The employer was Ismail, the present ex-Khedive of Egypt.

"England has taken a wet sponge and completely effaced this picture of successful development and attempt at civilization. Emin was clinging to the last floating spar of the general wreck when Stanley appeared upon the scene to his relief.

"Stanley's was not a Government expedition; it was the result of independent organization, with a special object, which was heroically attained; but there was no official plan for future operations. When Emin turned his back upon the Equatorial Province there was no British policy of re-occupation; the abandonment was complete, and the White Nile regions, including the Albert Nyanza, reverted to savagedom."

Baker did not take a hopeful view of the commercial advantages to be derived from an occupation of the regions he annexed and governed with such energy and spirit. He says:—"I should be sorry to invest any coin in the annexation of the Equatorial Province

A STORM ON THE ALBERT NYANZA.

with the expectation of seeing it again. During many years' experience in those parts I never saw any natural production worth one penny a pound, and the cost of transport to the coast would be a shilling, in the absence of the White Nile route and the line of steamers that we had established. Ivory cannot be purchased by legitimate means. The outlook commercially is not promising, but there is a grand field for adventure and for missionary enterprise in countries which have remained in savagedom since the time of the Creation, with a population that will fight and dance, but steadfastly refuse to work."

In the scramble for Africa, which set in about the time of the founding of the Congo State, a portion of the regions discovered by Livingstone was seized by the Germans, owing to the negligence of the Government, or a desire to conciliate that exacting people, who gave little in return for all our concessions.

Lakes Tanganyika and Nyassa were discovered by Burton and Livingstone, and the Stevenson Road, between these lakes, is the work of Englishmen, yet Germany laid claim to these parts, and divides with England the regions round Victoria Nyanza, discovered by Speke.

Germany demanded a portion of Ngamiland, discovered by Livingstone, and forgotten till the year 1890. It lies south of the Zambesi, on the limits of the German Protectorate of Damaraland. Its actual boundaries are: on the west, the twentieth degree; on the south, the twenty-second parallel; on the east, a line drawn from the point of intersection of the Chobe River and the Zambesi, which is about 50 miles west of the Victoria Falls, to the twenty-second parallel; and on the north, a line drawn from the same point of intersection, through Andara, to the twentieth degree. Within these limits is one of the most fertile districts in South Africa. The heart of it is the point marked on the maps as Lake Ngami. South of the lake the country is undulating, woody and well watered. It is also said to be very rich in minerals, and the climate is so good that Livingstone conceived the idea of making it a health resort for Central South Africa. The River Chobe is navigable only for canoes to the Zambesi, and the more important waterway of the Okavango rises in the neighborhood of the Cunene, in Portuguese territory, to the north, and passing southwards by Lake Ngami, changes its name to the Botletli (or Zuga), and runs out into the Kari Kari Lakes of Khama's country, within ten days' march of Shoshong. Ngamiland was formerly declared to be within the sphere of British influence when their Protectorate was announced over the neighboring country of Northern Bechuanaland.

Baker died in January, 1894. He was a stalwart, self-contained Englishman; a mighty hunter; a clear writer; an intelligent organizer, and an efficient executive, a noble specimen of a worthy race.

CHAPTER XII.

LIVINGSTONE'S LAST JOURNEYS AND DEATH.

NOTHWITHSTANDING the dangers and hardships he had endured during the many years spent in penetrating into the interior of Africa and exploring the Zambesi, Livingstone, unwearied and undaunted, felt an ardent desire to make further discoveries.

His previous expedition, "to promote the production of cotton, and to open up commercial enterprise," was substantially a failure. He was as keenly alive to this fact as any of his enemies. He had spent large sums of Government money, and all of his own, with results which caused general and outspoken dissatisfaction, and brought the whole subject of African exploration into disfavor.

He wished to resume his explorations, but lacked the means. Roderick Murchison and others interested themselves in his behalf, and got the Government to advance $2500. The Geographical Society advanced a further $2500, and $5000 more was subscribed by personal friends. Thus, before the end of 1865, Livingstone was once more in Africa, on a third expedition which lasted over seven years.

For the particulars of this expedition we have to

AMID THE REEDS OF LAKE BANGWEOLO.

depend on the brief letters he sent home at distant periods, and more especially on the deeply interesting account of Stanley, who made his adventurous journey to find him.

The Governor of Bombay gave Livingstone permission to take twelve Sepoys, who, being provided with Enfield rifles, were to act as guards to the expedition. He had brought nine men from Johanna, in the Comoro Islands, and these, with seven liberated slaves and two Zambesi men, making 30 in all, formed his attendants, who were considered sufficient to enable him to pass through the country without having to fear any plundering raids from the natives.

Leaving Zanzibar in March, 1866, he landed in a bay to the north of the Rovuma River early in the following month, and on April 7 he began his journey into the interior. His baggage consisted of bales of cloth and bags of beads, to enable him to purchase food and pay tribute to the chiefs through whose territories he might pass. He had, besides, his chronometer, sextant, artificial horizon and thermometers carried in cases, as also medicines, and the necessary clothing and other articles for himself. To carry the baggage he had six camels, three horses, two mules and three donkeys.

The route chosen was beset with difficulties. For miles on the banks of the river he found the country covered with dense jungle, through which the axe was required to hew a way.

Greatly to his disappointment the Sepoys and Johanna men, unused to such labor, showed a great dislike to it, and soon tried to frustrate the expedition, in order to compel their leader to return to the coast. So cruelly did they neglect and ill-treat the camels and other animals, that in a short time they all died. Natives were obtained to carry the loads.

Livingstone, feeling that should he be attacked, they would probably desert him, dismissed the Sepoys, and, sent them back to the coast.

For several days together he and his remaining men traveled through a wilderness, and, being unable to obtain food, they suffered much from hunger, while several of the men deserted. Thus was Livingstone left with only three or four attendants to prosecute his journey, while those who had gone off had robbed him of much of his property and even the greater part of his clothes.

Directing his course to the north-west, through the province of Londa, he reached the town of a chief named Kazembe. Londa, Kazembe's capital, is situated on the small Lake Mopo. To the north of it is a very much larger lake, called Moero.

This is only one of a series of lakes which Livingstone discovered in this portion of Central Africa. The most southern in the large Lake of Bangweolo, 4000 feet above the level of the sea, its area almost equal to that of Lake Tanganyika. It is into this lake that the Chambezi and a vast number of other smaller streams empty themselves.

The next important fact he observed was that a larger river than any of them, called the Luapula, runs out of the lake into Lake Moero. Out of the northern end of the Lake Moero again another large river, the Lualaba, runs thundering forth through a vast chasm, and then, expanding into a calm stream of great width, winds its way north and west till it enters a third large lake, the Kamolondo. To this was given the additional name of Webb's River. In some places it was found to be three miles broad. He followed it down its course, and found it again making its exit from Lake Kamolondo, till it was joined by other large rivers, some coming from the south and others from the east, till he reached the village of Nyangwé, in latitude 4° south. Here, having exhausted the means of purchasing fresh provisions, and his followers refusing to proceed farther, he was compelled to bring his journey northward to a termination. This was not till the year 1871.

Livingstone's discoveries entitle him to rank as, perhaps, the greatest of African explorers. All the ground he traversed during these years was virgin soil so far as the foot of the white man had traversed them. This place, Nyangwé, was the starting-point for a traveler equally eminent, whose fortunes were strangely linked with Livingstone's, in his remarkable journey down the Congo in 1874–77. In this journey Stanley proved, by following the river to its mouth, that the Lualaba of Livingstone, on which Nyangwé is situated, is the Congo, the second greatest river of Africa, and the course of which was the enigma of all ages.

He heard of another lake to the northward, into which, as he supposed, the Lualaba empties itself, bounded by a range to the westward, called the Balegga Mountains. From information received, he believed that this last-mentioned lake was connected by a series of small lakes, or by a somewhat sluggish stream, with the Albert Nyanza, the waters of which undoubtedly flow into the Nile.

To the south-west of Lake Kamolondo Livingstone discovered another large lake, to which he gave the name of Lincoln, after the President of the United States, the liberator of the negro slaves.

YOUNG BAMBARAS.

Another large river, the Lomane, flowing from the southward, enters this lake, and, passing out again at its northern end, joins the Luaba, which after that takes an almost northerly course. These important discoveries occupied Livingstone three years.

During his journeys, now to the west, now to the east, he met, in the latter quarter, a large sheet of water, which he discovered to be the southern end of Lake Tanganyika, and, after remaining some time with Kazembe, he set off, and crossed over to Ujiji, which he reached about the middle of March, 1869. After resting here till June, he again crossed the lake, and went westward with a party of traders till he reached the large village of Bambarra, in Manyuema. This is the chief ivory depôt in that province, where large quantities are obtained.

He was here detained six months, suffering severely from ulcers in his feet, which prevented him putting them to the ground, and from thence it was, when again able to set out, that he tracked for a certain distance the course of the Lualaba, which occupied him till the year 1871.

From Nyangwé, he returned eastward to Ujiji, a distance of 700 miles. Ruo, in which he discovered copper mines, lies directly to the south of it. Each village is governed by its own chief, holding little or no communication with its neighbors. They possess a considerable amount of ingenuity, and manufacture a fabric from fine grass, equal to the finest grass cloth of India.

Livingstone describes the people as of light color, with well-formed features. Being of gentle manners, the women are eagerly sought for by the Arabs, whose wives they sometimes become.

On reaching Ujiji, on October 16, 1871, greatly to his dismay he found that his agent, believing him to be dead, had sold all the goods for ivory, which he had appropriated.

Thus Livingstone, already suffering fearfully from illness, found himself deprived of the means of purchasing food or paying his way back to the coast. The letters, stores and provisions sent to him from Zanzibar had been detained on the road, but relief, when least expected, was at hand.

It has been mentioned that, in the year 1866, his followers deserted him and then made for the coast, where they at once spread the report that Livingstone had been murdered by the sanguinary tribe of Mazitu.

We know that this tale was false, for we have already tracked the doctor to Ujiji, but the authorities at Zanzibar, in 1866, had no such evidence. Musa stated supposed facts in a very circumstantial manner, and rumors thus circulated gave rise to the activity which resulted in the Search Expeditions despatched from England; which, however, were rendered abortive by the enterprise of the *New York Herald* and its correspondent, Henry M. Stanley.

The news of Livingstone's murder was received in England with sorrow. The story had so many elements of apparent truth in its composition, that friends and relatives feared the worst.

But some people discredited the news; and it was suggested that an expedition should be despatched to find the explorer, but this proposal was combated as one which, if carried out, would prove useless and disastrous.

After some months had elapsed, his adherents gained

their point. A former companion of Livingstone, Edward D. Young, was appointed leader, and proceeded from the Cape in June, 1867, to the mouth of the Zambesi, where a small steel vessel, named the *Search*, was successfully launched upon the waters of the great river.

After some adventures, and a visit to a Portuguese settlement, whose chief gave the members confirmation of Livingstone's death—which, however, Young did not credit—the *Search* continued her course, and entered the Shiré River. Here they were attacked by the natives, but, on being recognized as English, were hospitably received, and everywhere, as the little party continued their route, the inhabitants recognized the English as old friends.

Information coming in from time to time, assured Young that he was on the right trail. No hostile tribe opposed their progress, and the *Search* continued her venturesome way unmolested. At length, in the beginning of September, 1867, Nyassa Lake was gained, and it became now a difficult matter to decide in what direction the course should be steered. A "white man" had been reported as having gone in a northwesterly direction, but that was long ago, and Young and his men were somewhat undecided.

The appearance of a native, however, gave them hope; on being questioned, enough was learned to assure Young that, so far, he had been proceeding in the right direction, and that Livingstone had certainly not been murdered.

Proceeding up the lake, the good news was confirmed. The illustrious traveler had remained in a small village by the water during the past winter

LOANDA.

season, and had left an excellent impression upon the natives.

Doubt could no longer exist in the minds of the members of the *Search* party that they had found "warm" traces of the great explorer. Further inquiries resulted in information respecting his observations of the sun with the sextant—which were illustrated by means of sticks—by a detail of the number of his men, "two or three tens" of persons, his feet clothed in "skins" (boots)—and his little dog was mentioned.

Mr. Young at once continued his course, crossing the lake to Chivola, where more relics and reminiscences of the doctor were discovered and related. The villagers gave many faithful and interesting details of the white man's residence with them, and held his memory in great reverence, for he and his countrymen set their faces against slave-dealing.

A native, who was encountered by the lake, gave the valuable intelligence that he had himself seen and assisted Livingstone, after the desertion of Musa and his faithless companions. The man scouted the idea of Livingstone having been murdered, and Musa's ingenious fabrication of the death and burial was fully proved false when the *Search* party penetrated to the Babisa country, and interviewed the old chief.

Young came to the conclusion that Livingstone was alive, and that he had wandered through territories infested by a hostile tribe, who had destroyed the villages. The Babisa chief warmly dissuaded Young from attempting to follow, and accordingly, the *Search* expedition returned to the coast, and to England, with the information they had acquired.

DRAGGING A STEAMER THROUGH THE VEGETATION.

Though nothing definite had actually been heard of the great explorer since May, 1869, Murchison expressed his belief in Livingstone's existence. He had been reported at Ujiji, on Lake Tanganyika, where he was waiting supplies. Samuel Baker hoped to find him, but this hope had no actual result, owing to geographical difficulties.

A relief expedition was now proposed. Money was subscribed throughout England, and the Geographical Society took the matter in hand for the nation. Lieutenants Dawson and Henn were selected as the leaders, from a list of 400 volunteers. Oswell Livingstone went with them.

The Livingstone Search Expedition landed at Zanzibar on March 17, 1872, and made their preparations for advancing. On April 27, Lieutenants Henn and Dawson were about to start, when three men came in who had been sent on by a person, named Stanley, with the announcement that Livingstone had been found. Livingstone had sent certain instructions by Stanley, and there was nothing to be done but despatch to his aid the men and stores he required.

CHAPTER XIII.

Stanley's Expedition in Search of Livingstone.

HENRY MORTON STANLEY, who found and relieved Livingstone, and has since performed the more arduous task of succoring Emin Pasha, is one of the most remarkable men of the century. To be a successful traveler demands uncommon qualities, but Stanley possesses them all in a degree so marked, that he may well be called the "Prince of African Travelers," and the name deservedly applied to him by Burton has, with characteristic generosity, been conceded to this world-renowned explorer.

At the time Stanley proceeded to Abyssinia as the correspondent of the *New York Herald*, he was a naturalized citizen of the United States, and the traveler encouraged the belief that he was an American by birth, and always called himself an American. But his birth, antecedents, and early life have all been ferreted out by a public which demands to know every particular of its great men, and it has been ascertained that Stanley is a Welshman.

He was born in the year 1840, and his name is John Rowlands. Like many celebrated characters, including travelers, such as Livingstone and the Landers, Stanley, as we must continue to call him, was of humble origin.

His mother was left a widow when he was only two years of age, and he was placed in the workhouse school of St. Asaph, near to which he was born. There he remained for ten years, and though little is known of his early life, it has been ascertained that he was remarkable at school for intelligence and determination of character, characteristics which he displayed throughout his career.

He ran away from school, and finding his way to Liverpool, worked his passage on a sailing ship bound for New Orleans. Arrived here he found employment in the office of a gentleman named Stanley, who took a fancy to him, and adopted him. Thus John Rowlands became Henry Morton Stanley, a name known throughout the civilized world, and even in the pathless forests and wilds of Africa.

But now a misfortune befell him. His kind employer and benefactor died suddenly, and, having made no will, his property was claimed by his relatives, and Stanley found himself once more thrown on the world, with nothing to aid him but his indomitable will. When the American Civil War broke out, Stanley joined the Confederate Army, under General Johnston, and was engaged in some of the battles until he became a prisoner at Pittsburg Landing. He managed, however, to escape by swimming across a river, and subsequently made his way to England. But the great Republic had a superior fascination for one of his adventurous tastes, and again he worked his passage out, this time to New York. Stanley now transferred his allegiance to the Northern States, and served in the Federal Navy until the close of the war, when he joined, as a newspaper correspondent, an expedition against the Indians in the Far West,

(155)

and, on his return, was taken on the staff of the *New York Herald*.

In this capacity, he served through the Abyssinian War, and by his enterprise anticipated his fellows in an account of the capture of Magdala. He was correspondent of the *New York Herald* in the Carlist War, in Spain, and, in the years 1873-74, in the brief and arduous Ashantee campaign.

But before this last service, Stanley undertook his expedition for the discovery and relief of Livingstone, which first brought him prominently before the world. The circumstances of his appointment are sufficiently singular and amusing to be recorded. Stanley was at Madrid on October 16, 1869, when he received a telegram from James Gordon Bennett, proprietor of the *New York Herald*, to join him at Paris. He thus records the interview with Mr. Bennett on his arrival at his hotel at Paris :—

"I went straight to the 'Grand Hotel,' and knocked at the door of, Mr. Bennett's room.

"'Come in,' I heard a voice say. Entering I found Mr. Bennett in bed.

"'Who are you?' he asked.

"'My name is Stanley,' I answered.

"'Ah, yes, sit down. I have important business in hand for you. Where do you think Livingstone is?'

"'I really do not know, sir.'

"'Do you think he is alive?'

"'He may be, and he may not be,' I answered.

"'Well, I think he is alive, and that he can be found; and I am going to send you to find him. Of course, you can act according to your own plans, and do what you think best; but find Livingstone!'"

When Stanley spoke of the expense, Mr. Bennett said:—

"Draw a thousand pounds now, and when you have gone through that, draw another thousand, and when that is spent, draw another thousand, and when you have finished that, draw another thousand, and so on; but find Livingstone!"

Stanley's instructions were, first, to ascertain in Egypt what Samuel Baker—then about to start up the Nile—intended to do, and then to make his way, via Bombay and Mauritius, to Zanzibar.

He arrived on January 6, 1871, at Zanzibar, and without delay set about making the preparations for his journey into the interior of the African Continent.

He had engaged at Jerusalem a Christian Arab boy, named Selim, who was to act as his interpreter, and he had also on the voyage attached to the expedition two mates of merchantmen, Farquhar and Shaw, who were useful in constructing tents and arranging two boats for the journey. He also secured the services of Bombay, captain of Speke's "faithfuls," and five of his other followers, Uledi, Grant's valet, and Mabruki, who had in the meantime lost one of his hands. They were the only remains of the band to be found, the rest having died or gone elsewhere.

The boats, one of which was capable of carrying 20 people, and the other six, were stripped of their planks, the timbers and thwarts only being carried. Instead of the planking it was proposed to cover them with double canvas skin, well tarred. They and the rest of the baggage were carried in loads, none exceeding 68 pounds in weight. Two horses and 27 donkeys were purchased, and a small cart, while the traveler had brought with him a watch-dog, which he hoped would guard his tent from prowling thieves. An ample supply of beads, cloth and wire were also laid in, with tea, sugar, rice, and medicine. To Bombay and his "faithfuls" were added 18 more freemen, well armed, who were to act as escort to the carriers.

On February 5, 1871, the expedition embarked in four dhows, which conveyed it across to Bagamoyo on the mainland. Here it was detained five weeks, while its leader was struggling to overcome the rogueries of the Arabs, who had undertaken to secure 140 porters, and in making the necessary arrangements. At Bagamoyo he found a caravan which had been despatched by the British Consul 100 days before to the relief of Livingstone; but which had hitherto remained inactive, its leader making an excuse that he was unable to obtain a fresh supply of carriers.

Stanley divided his expedition into five caravans, the first of which he started off on February 18, although it was not till March 21, 1871, that he, with the largest, was able to begin his journey westward. Altogether the expedition numbered on the day of departure, besides the commander and his two white attendants, 23 soldiers, four chiefs, and 154 carriers. Every care had been bestowed on the outfit, which was deemed complete.

Bombay proved to be as honest and trustworthy as formerly, while Ferajji and Mabruki turned out true men and staunch, the latter on one occasion, finding a difficulty in dragging the cart, having brought it along on his head rather than abandon it.

The Kingani River was crossed by a bridge rapidly formed with American axes, the donkeys refusing to pass through the water.

Few men were better able to deal with the rogueries of the petty chiefs he met with than Stanley. He had always a ready answer, and caught them in their own traps, while the "great master," as he was called, managed to keep all his subordinates in good order.

Before long Stanley was attacked with fever, which greatly prostrated his strength, though he quickly recovered by taking strong doses of quinine.

The report from Farquhar's caravan was most unsatisfactory, he, as far as Stanley could make out, having lost all his donkeys. The unhappy man was suffering from dropsy, and had to be sent back.

The expedition was now about to enter Ugogo. During the passage of the intervening desert, five out of the nine donkeys died, the cart having some time before been left behind. The expedition was now joined by several Arab caravans, so that the number of the party amounted to about 400 souls, strong in guns, flags, horns, sounding drums, and noise. This host was to be led by Stanley and Hamed through the dreaded Ugogo.

On May 26, they were at Mvumi, paying heavy tribute to the Sultan. While here five more donkeys died, and their bones were picked clean before the morning by the hyenas.

The tribute was paid to preserve peace, and the party proceeded westward. The country was one vast field of grain, and thickly populated. Between that place and the next Sultan's district, 25 villages were counted.

After this wearisome journey Stanley was again attacked by fever, which it required a whole day's halt and fifty grains of quinine to cure. As may be supposed, they were thankful when Ugogo was passed, and they entered Unyanyembe.

The expedition at length entered Kivihara, the capital of the province ruled over by the aged Sultan Mkaswa, who received Stanley in a friendly way. The Sheik Said Ben Salim invited him to take up his quarters in his house, where Stanley's goods were stored and his carriers paid off. His three other caravans had arrived safely.

Soon after, the Livingstone caravan arrived, and the goods were stored with those of Stanley, the men being quartered with his. The chief of the caravan brought Stanley a package of letters directed to Livingstone at Ujiji.

After his long journey, Stanley was completely prostrate, and for two weeks was perfectly senseless. Selim, who had faithfully watched over his master and treated him according to the written directions he received, was also prostrated, and in a state of delirium for four days.

On July 28, 1871, all had again recovered, and on the next day, 50 carriers were ready to start.

The road ahead was closed by the chief Mirambo, who declared that no Arab caravan should pass that way. The Arabs, therefore, had resolved to attack him, and mustered an army of upwards of 2000 men. Stanley, with his followers, determined to join them, to assist in bringing the war to a speedy conclusion.

The palace was soon surrounded, and, though the party were received with a volley, the fire of the defenders was soon silenced. They took to flight, and the village was entered. Notwithstanding the heavy fire which had been kept up on it, 20 dead bodies only were found. Other villages were attacked and burned.

A more serious affair occurred soon afterwards.

When Stanley was again attacked with fever, a number of his men, notwithstanding his orders to the contrary, joined the Arabs in an attack on a more important place, commanded by Mirambo himself. The result was that, though the place was taken, the Arabs fell into an ambush, laid by Mirambo, and were completely defeated, many of them, including some of Stanley's soldiers, being killed. Mirambo, following up his successes, pursued the Arabs, and Stanley had to mount his donkey, Shaw being lifted on his, and to fly at midnight for their lives. His soldiers ran as fast as their legs could carry them, the only one of his followers who remained by his master's side being young Selim. At length they reached Mfuto, from which they had issued forth so valiantly a short time before.

Stanley had felt it his duty to assist the Arabs, though he had now cause to regret having done so. He returned to Kivihara. Here he was detained a long time, during which he received authentic news of Livingstone from an Arab, who had met with him traveling into Manyuema, and who affirmed that, having gone to a market at Liemba in three canoes, one of them, in which all his cloth had been placed, was upset and lost. The news of Farquhar's death here reached him.

Month after month passed away, and he had great difficulty in obtaining soldiers to supply the places of those who had been killed or died. One day he received a present of a little slave boy from an Arab merchant, to whom, at Bombay's suggestion, the name of Kalulu, meaning a young antelope, was given.

Stanley was again attacked with fever, but his white companion in no degree sympathized with him, even little Kalulu showing more feeling. Weak as he was, he again began his march to the westward, with about 40 men added to his old followers.

Bombay, not for the first time, proving refractory and impudent, received a thrashing before starting, and when Stanley arrived at his camp at night, he found that upwards of twenty men had remained behind. He sent a strong body back, under Selim, who returned with the men and some heavy slave-chains, and Stanley declared that if any behaved in the same way again he would fasten them together and make them march like slaves.

As war was going on in the country, it was necessary to proceed with caution. Some of his followers showed a strong inclination to mutiny, which he had to quell by summary proceedings, and Bombay especially sank greatly in his good opinion. As they approached Lake Tanganyika, all got into better humor, and confidence was restored between them.

On November 2, 1871, the left bank of the Malagarazi River was reached. The greater part of the day had been occupied in dealing with the chief of the greedy Wavinza tribe, who demanded an enormous sum. This being settled, the ferrymen asked payment for carrying across the caravan. These demands having been settled, the next business was to swim the donkeys across. One fine animal was being towed with a rope round its neck, when, just as it reached the middle of the stream, it was seen to struggle fearfully. An enormous crocodile had seized the poor animal by the throat. The black in charge tugged at the rope, but the donkey sank and was no more seen. Only one donkey now remained, and this was taken across by Bombay the next morning.

The next day was an eventful one. Just before starting, a caravan was seen approaching, consisting of a

"DR. LIVINGSTONE, I PRESUME?"

large party of a tribe occupying a tract of country to the south-west of Lake Tanganyika.

The news was asked. A white man had been seen by them who had lately arrived at Ujiji from Manyuema. He had white hair and a white beard, and was sick. Only eight days ago they had seen him. He had been at Ujiji before, and had gone away and returned. There could be no doubt that this was Livingstone.

Stanley started in high spirits, pushing on as fast as his men could move. On November 10, just 236 days after leaving Bagomoyo, and 51 since they set out from Unyanyembe, surmounting a hill, the Lake of Tanganyika was seen before them. Six hours' march brought them to its shores.

The "stars and stripes" were given to the breeze; and repeated volleys were fired. The faithful Chumah and Susi, Livingstone's old followers, rushed out of the village to see the stranger, and in a short time Stanley was rewarded for all the dangers and hardships he had undergone by greeting the long-looked-for traveler face to face. The meeting of these two remarkable men has become historical. Stanley, advancing, held out his hand, with the words, "Dr. Livingstone, I presume;" and the travel-worn, but indomitable explorer replied simply in the affirmative.

At this time, when reduced almost to death's door by sickness and disappointment, the assistance thus brought to Livingstone was of inestimable worth. The society of his new friend, the letters from home, the well-cooked meal which the doctor was able to enjoy, and the champagne quaffed out of silver goblets, brought carefully those hundreds of miles for that especial object, had a wonderfully exhilarating influence.

Some days were spent at Ujiji, during which Livingstone regained health and strength. Future plans were discussed, and his previous adventures described. The longer the intercourse Stanley enjoyed with Livingstone, the more he rose in his estimation.

"Dr. Livingstone," he says, "is about sixty years old. His hair has a brownish color, but here and there streaked with grey lines over the temples. His beard and moustache are very grey. His eyes, which are hazel, are remarkably bright: he has a sight keen as a hawk's. His frame is a little over the ordinary height; when walking, he has a firm but heavy tread, like that of an over-worked or fatigued man. I never observed any spleen or misanthropy about him. He has a fund of quiet humor, which he exhibits at all times when he is among friends. During the four months I was with him I noticed him every evening making most careful notes. His maps evince great care and industry. He is sensitive on the point of being doubted or criticised. His gentleness never forsakes him, his hopefulness never deserts him; no harassing anxiety or distraction of mind, though separated from home and kindred, can make him complain. He thinks all will come out right at last, he has such faith in the goodness of Providence. Another thing which especially attracted my attention was his wonderfully retentive memory. His religion is not of the theoretical kind, but it is constant, earnest, sincere, practical; it is neither demonstrative nor loud, but manifests itself in a quiet, practical way, and is always at work. In him religion exhibits its loveliest features; it governs his conduct not only towards his servants, but towards the natives. I observed that universal respect was paid to him; even the Mohammedans never passed his house without calling to pay their compliments, and to say: '.The blessing of God rest on you!' Every Sunday morning he gathers his little flock around him, and reads prayers and a chapter from the Bible in a natural, unaffected, and sincere tone, and afterwards delivers a short address in the Kiswahili language, about the subject read to them, which is listened to with evident interest and attention.

"His consistent energy is native to him and his race. He is a very fine example of the perseverance, doggedness and tenacity which characterize the Anglo-Saxon spirit. His ability to withstand the climate is due not only to the happy constitution with which he was born, but to the strictly temperate life he has ever led."

In another place Stanley says: " Livingstone followed the dictates of duty. Never was such a willing slave to that abstract virtue. Surely, as the sun shines on both Christian and infidel, civilized and pagan, the day of enlightenment will come: and though the apostle of Africa may not behold it himself, nor we younger men, nor yet our children, the hereafter will see it, and posterity will recognize the daring pioneer of its civilization."

After they had been some weeks together at Ujiji, Stanley and Livingstone agreed to make a voyage on Lake Tanganyika, one of the chief objects of which was to settle the long-mooted point as to whether the Rusizi River is an affluent or an effluent. They embarked in a cranky canoe, hollowed out of a tree, which carried 16 rowers, Selim, and two guides, besides themselves.

The lake was calm, its waters of a dark green color, reflecting the serene blue sky above. At one place where they sounded, the depth was found to be 210 feet near the shore, and farther out 350 feet of line was let down without finding bottom, and Dr. Livingstone stated that he had sounded opposite the lofty Kabogo, and attained the depth of 1800 feet.

We will not venture to attempt a description of the magnificent scenery of this enormous lake. Each night they landed and encamped, continuing their voyage the next day. Generally they were well received by the natives, though they had to avoid one or two spots where the people were said to be treacherous and quarrelsome. On reaching the mouth of the Rusizi, they pushed up it a short distance, but found that it was navigable only for the smallest canoes.

The most important point, however, which they discovered was that the current was flowing, at the rate of six to eight miles an hour, *into* the lake.

Coasting round the north shore, they paddled down the west coast till nearly opposite the island of Muzimu, when they crossed back to the shore from whence they had come, and steered southward beyond Ujiji till they reached nearly the sixth degree of latitude, at a place called Urimba. Their voyage, altogether, took 28 days, during which time they traversed over 300 miles of water.

On their return to Ujiji, they resolved to carry out one of the several plans which Stanley had suggested to Livingstone. One of them was to return to Unyanyembe to enlist men to sail down the Victoria Nyanza in Stanley's boat, for the purpose of meeting Samuel Baker; but this, with several others, was dismissed. Livingstone's heart was set on endeavoring to settle numerous important points in Manyuema connected with the supposed source of the Nile. He finally agreed to allow Stanley to escort him to Unyanyembe, where he should receive his own goods and those which Stanley proposed to deliver up to him, and where he could rest in a comfortable house, while his friend would hurry down the coast, and organize a new expedition, composed of 60 men, well armed, by. whom an additional supply of needful luxuries might be sent.

Christmas Day was kept up with such a feast as Ujiji could furnish them, the fever from which Stanley had lately been suffering having left him the night before.

On December 27, 1871, they embarked in two canoes, the one bearing the flag of England, the other that of America; and their baggage being on board, and having bidden farewell to Arabs and natives, together they commenced their voyage on the lake, steering for the south. At the same time the main body of their men began their journey, which was to be performed on foot, along the shores of the lake. It had been arranged that the canoes should meet them at the mouth of every river, to transport them across from bank to bank. Their intention was to land at Cape Tongwe, when they would be opposite the village of Itaga, whence by traversing the uninhabited districts to the east, they would avoid the exactions of the roguish Wavinza and the plundering Wahha, and then strike the road by which Stanley had come. This plan was completely carried out. Stanley had procured a strong donkey at Ujiji, that Livingstone might perform the journey on its back.

Pouring rain came down during the whole journey, and it was to their intense satisfaction that at length the two friends walked into Stanley's old quarters, who said, "Doctor, we are at home."

Here they were again busily employed in examining

stores, and Livingstone in writing despatches and letters to his friends. Here he resolved to remain, while Stanley went down to the coast to enlist men and collect such further stores as were required, and to send them back. On their arrival he purposed returning with them to Ujiji, and from thence crossing over into Manyuema, to make further researches in that province and Ruo; among other things, to examine the underground habitations which he had heard of on a previous journey.

On March 14, 1872, Stanley and Livingstone breakfasted together, and then the order was given to raise the flag and march. Livingstone accompanied him some way, but they had to part at last.

The return journey was not performed without many adventures and a considerable amount of suffering by the enterprising traveler.

Passing the stronghold of Kisalungo, a large portion had disappeared. The river had swept away the entire front wall and about 50 houses, several villages having suffered disastrously, while at least 100 people had perished. The whole valley, once a paradise in appearance, had been converted into a howling waste. Farther on, a still more terrible destruction of human life and property had occurred. It was reported that 100 villages had been swept away by the inundation of a river. Passing a dense jungle, and wading for several miles through a swamp, on May 6, the caravan was again *en route* at a pace its leader had never seen equalled. At sunset the town of Bagamoyo was entered.

His first greeting was with Lieutenant Henn, who had come out as second in command of the proposed Livingstone Search and Relief Expedition. He next met Oswell Livingstone. The two proposed shortly starting on their journey, having come over with no less than 190 loads of stores, which they would have had no small difficulty in conveying. Stanley was not overwell pleased with some of the remarks made in the papers about himself, some having regarded his expedition into Africa as a myth.

"Alas!" he observes, "it has been a terrible, earnest fact with me: nothing but hard, conscientious work, privations, sickness and almost death."

However, welcomed cordially by numerous friends at Zanzibar, he soon recovered his spirits, and, having disbanded his own expedition, set to work to arrange the one he had promised to form for the assistance of Livingstone, Mr. Henn having in the meantime resigned, and Oswell Livingstone being compelled from ill health to abandon the attempt to join his father.

Fifty rifles, with ammunition, stores and cloth, were furnished by Oswell Livingstone out of the English expedition. 57 men, including 20 of those who had followed Stanley, were also engaged, the services of Johari, chief dragoman to the American consulate, being also obtained to conduct them across the inundated plains of the Kingani.

Having engaged a dhow, Stanley saw them all on board, and again urged them to follow the "great master," as they called Livingstone, wherever he might lead them, and to obey him in all things. He then shook hands with them, and, watched the dhow as she sped westward on her way to Bagamoyo.

Those who had accompanied him were rewarded, and he states to their credit, though Bombay and many others had at first annoyed him greatly, that from Ujiji to the coast, they had all behaved admirably.

Dr. Livingstone, in parting with Stanley, stated that he did not intend to return home until he had satisfied himself concerning the sources of the Nile. He expressed his determination to strike across country from Lake Tanganyika to the Lualaba River. "Crossing that," he continued, "I will go to the Katanga mines," and eight days south of the Katanga, the natives had assured the explorer the "fountains of the Nile" were to be found. The doctor proposed to return from Katanga, then journey to Lake Komolondo, up the Lufira to Lake Lincoln. Coming down again, he would proceed by the Lualaba to the next lake, and then make his way to Zanzibar, which he estimated would occupy him a year and a half.

"May God bring you back safe to us all, my dear friend," was Stanley's last wish. "Farewell."

Stanley sent the men and the supplies for two years to Livingstone, who waited for them until August, at Unyanyembe, where Stanley had left him. On August 25, 1872, the little caravan, which numbered 60 persons, including many faithful adherents, quitted Unyanyembe upon Livingstone's last journey towards the eastern shore of Lake Tanganyika. The expedition proceeded without any very remarkable incident occurring till, on September 15, we find the significant entry in the journal, which on that day closes with the word "Ill." Nevertheless next day Livingstone passed over the range of hills, and then westward to the village of Kamirambo. On the 18th, the party "remained at Miriras," and Livingstone's old foe (dysentery) attacked him, and afterwards his followers spoke of few periods of health.

But the explorer still pressed on, with occasional halts for rest, and on October 8, he "came on early, as the sun was hot, and in two hours saw the Tanganyika from a gentle hill." After a short rest, Livingstone proceeded along the top of the range, which runs parallel with the lake about 1000 feet above it. Then, crossing several inlets of the lake, the party proceeded through a country swarming with game, and so on over the hills and mountains; then southwards. After suffering from want of food, and by the falseness of a guide, the expedition climbed up a steep mountain, whence a view of the lake was obtained. They descended to the valley; and on the 12th and 13th, their journey led them over low ranges of sandstone, past several stockaded villages, and they arrived at Zombé's Town.

The loss of the best donkey is recorded as a calamity. So the journey continued with varying daily progress till the Lofu was reached on November 28, 1872, and subsequently the Lower Katanta, through heavy rains and many streams. Food was scarce; while the entries in the journal show that the doctor was feeble and ailing.

Christmas Day was cold and wet, but a day of rest and some rejoicing. They pushed on again, in wet and drizzling weather, till on January 8, 1873, they were detained by heavy rains at Moenje. "We are near Lake Bangweolo," says Livingstone, "and in a damp region." Thenceforward it appears that the journey was a continual plunge into and out of morasses, "and through rivers which were only distinguishable from the surrounding waters by their deep currents, and the necessity for using canoes." To a man reduced in strength, and chronically affected with dysenteric symptoms ever likely to be aggravated by exposure, the effect may well be conceived.

CROSSING ON THE ATTENDANT'S SHOULDERS.

173

A dry day enabled the caravan to "move forward an hour to a rivulet and sponge"—through flat forest, "to a running rivulet with one hundred yards of sponge on each side." There was a great want of canoes, and no assistance was afforded by the natives. Sometimes Livingstone was carried across the rivulets; for he was too weak to wade, and thus, in a continued series of troubles and worries, the painful pilgrimage was continued. An entry, under date of January 24, with an illustration, in the "Journal," tells us the extreme difficulty of the passage. Plunging through a stream, neck deep, in pouring rain, he was passed from one pair of shoulders to another for fifty yards at a time. A terrible journey indeed, and nothing but the greatest pluck and determination, united with respect for the leader, could have kept the people together.

So February passed, and March found them on a miserable island. "We are surrounded by scores of miles of rushes, an open sward, and many lotus plants, but no mosquitoes," adds the diarist, thankfully.

Still wandering in the swamps of Lake Bangweolo, the explorer continued his search for evidence of the junction of the Lualaba with the Lake; but doubt of success seems to have filled the doctor's mind. "Can I hope for ultimate success?" he writes on March 19; "so many obstacles have arisen!" This was Livingstone's last birthday, when, perhaps, the shadow of the coming darkness was perceptible to his mind.

At length, in the beginning of April, the complaint from which he had been so long suffering assumed a bad character, and left him "bloodless and weak, from bleeding profusely since March 31. Oh! how I long to be permitted by the Over Power to finish my work." This

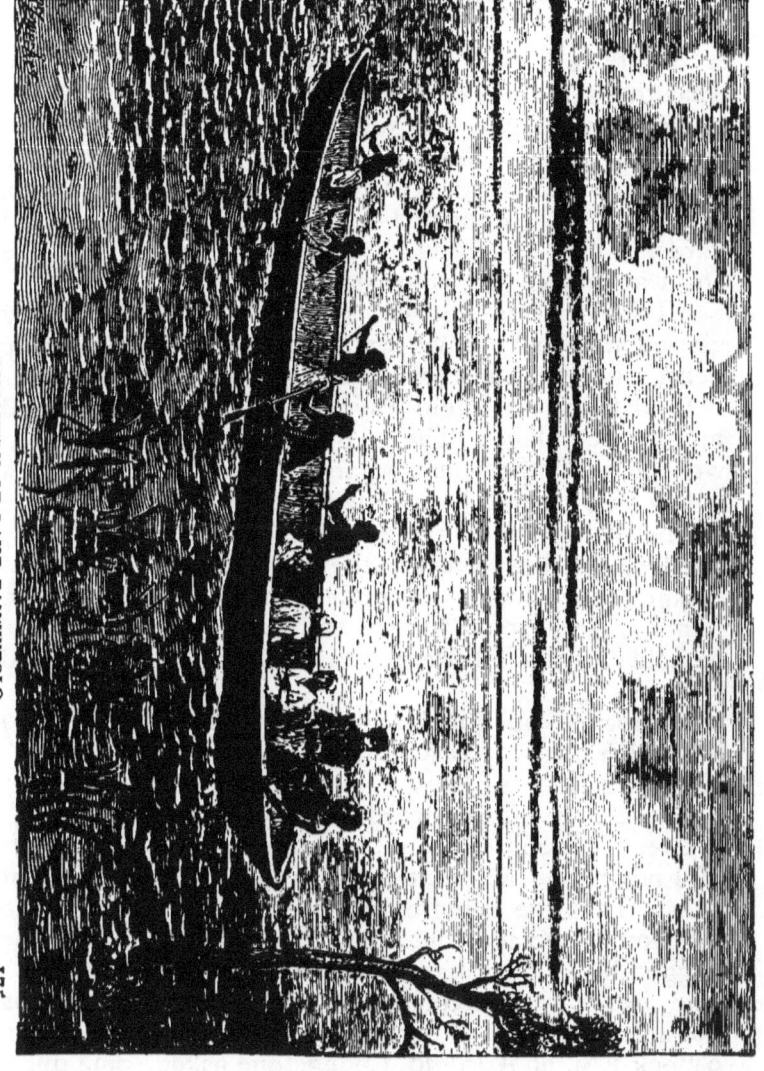

DISCOVERY OF LAKE BANGWEOLO.

entry tells us, more than many pages of description, what the sufferings of the brave man were. On April 12 he adds, " Lay down quite done, cooked coffee—our last—and went on, but in an hour I was compelled to lie down." The 19th tells us: " I am excessively weak, and but for the donkey I could not move a hundred yards. *It is not all pleasure, this exploration!*" The end was, indeed, drawing near.

"Tried to ride, but was forced to lie down. They carried me back to vil. exhausted." Fight on, brave heart, fight on, but it is in vain. Chuma and Susi, his faithful followers, undid Livingstone's belt, and carried him to the village. The men perceived the increasing weakness of their master, and made him a litter, in which they carried him, suffering acutely.

Then only dates are entered. Passing through the flooded, treeless wastes, the men were sheltered in villages, the doctor becoming weaker and weaker. Sunday, April 20, 1873, was the date of the last service he held with his followers, and on the 27th he appeared to be dying.

"Knocked up quite, and remain—recover—sent to buy milch goats. We are on the banks of the Molilamo" (Lulimala).

These were the last words Livingstone ever wrote.

Great difficulties were encountered in the transport of Livingstone across the river, for he was in great pain. Then the dying explorer was carried forward to Chitumbo's village, but even in this brief transit he begged his bearers many times to stop and let him rest. The house was erected and made ready as soon as possible, and the litter placed within it. At eleven o'clock P. M. on April 30, Livingstone asked some ques-

THE LAST MILE OF LIVINGSTONE'S TRAVELS.

tions of his attendant, Susi, and then dozed off. An hour later Susi was again called, and Livingstone took some medicine. "All right; you can go now," he said. And Susi left him.

Early on the morning of May 1, a lad came to Susi and called him to "Bwana," for "I don't know if he is alive!" Susi, alarmed, ran to fetch the rest.

A candle stuck by its own wax to the top of the box shed a light sufficient for them to see his form. Livingstone was kneeling by the side of his bed, his body stretched forward, his head buried in his hands upon the pillow. For a minute they watched him; he did not stir; there was no sign of breathing; then one of them, Matthew, advanced softly to him and placed his hands to his cheeks. It was sufficient; life had been extinct some time, and the body was almost cold: Livingstone was dead.

The heart of Livingstone was buried where he died, his body was preserved by being fully exposed to the sun and then was reverently conveyed by his faithful servants to Zanzibar, whence it was transferred to England, and placed, with stately ceremonies and amid crowds of mourners, with the remains of the greatest and noblest of the English race who sleep in the Abbey of Westminster.

The coffin bore this inscription—

DAVID LIVINGSTONE.

Born at Blantyre, Lanarkshire, Scotland,

19 MARCH, 1813,

Died at Ilala, Central Africa,

1 MAY, 1873.

CHAPTER XIV.

Cameron's Journey Across Africa.

Lieutenant Verney Cameron, of the British Navy, volunteered, in the year 1872, to conduct an expedition to explore the region which Livingstone had traversed, and in which he had so long lived.

Cameron, accompanied by Dr. Dillon, a former messmate, reached Zanzibar in January, 1873. He declared his purpose of crossing Africa from sea to sea, and this he accomplished. But his party was not a very strong one, for only 30 men were collected, and Bombay, who had the selection, took no trouble in the matter.

In February, 1873, the expedition marched into the interior without impediment, and reached Killoa without having encountered any important adventure by the way. Cameron had meantime been joined by R. Moffat, a nephew of Doctor Livingstone, who was left with Lieutenant Murphy.

The journey from Killoa was most enervating—across the swamps and the terrible Makata morass, where Dr. Dillon was taken ill, and could go no farther. Cameron, however, pushed on into higher and more healthy country, and at once sent back assistance and conveyance for his friend, who was conveyed to Rehenucko.

The march to Unyanyembe was accomplished under

the greatest difficulties. Death, desertion and suffering marked the course with sad milestones, as day by day the route was pursued. But in August, 1873, the place so famous in African travel, from the time when Burton and Speke first entered it, was gained.

At Unyanyembe, Cameron met with a kind welcome, and was installed in the same dwelling which had already sheltered Livingstone and Stanley. But once again trouble arose with the men. A mutiny broke out, which was quelled, but fever and desertion decimated the following of Cameron and Dillon. The head man, Bombay, already mentioned, gave himself up to the habit of intoxication; while, to add to the trouble, Cameron himself suffered from a severe attack of fever, which nearly proved fatal.

This was a trying time, and in the letters written by Dillon may be found the affecting record of the young leader's sufferings and delirium in that fearful fever which soon was to lay its fell grasp upon Dillon himself, and caused him to die by his own hand in a paroxysm of madness. During many weary weeks Cameron remained prostrate, but October found him on the road to convalescence.

October 20 brought in news of a very saddening nature. As Cameron was slowly recovering, his servant entered the tent and gave him a letter which had just arrived. The man could tell nothing more than it had come in by a messenger.

The letter, of which we give a literal copy, was from Jacob Wainright to Oswell Livingstone.

" SIR :—We have heard, in the month of August, that you have started from Zanzibar for Unyanyembe,

and, again, have lately heard of your arrival. Your father died by disease beyond the country of Bisa, but we have carried the corpse with us. Ten of our soldiers are lost, and some have died. Our hunger presses us to ask of you some clothes to buy provisions for our soldiers, and we should have an answer that, when we shall enter, there shall be firing guns or not; and, if you will permit us to fire guns, then send us some powder. We have written these few words in the place of Sultan or King Mborwa.
"The Writer,
"JACOB WAINWRIGHT,
"Dr. Livingstone Expedition."

This was the first intimation of the death of the celebrated African explorer, and it fell upon eyes and ears dimmed and dulled by fever. Dillon and Cameron, both only half recovered, took some time to grasp the meaning; but on the arrival of the faithful Chumah, all doubt of the fact was put an end to. Cameron's occupation was virtually gone! The Livingstone Search Expedition had been arrested by the hand of death. Cameron and his companions might now return, for their mission had been accomplished.

But Cameron determined to proceed across the continent westwards, while Dillon and Murphy accompanied the funeral procession of Dr. Livingstone, as already related. Poor Dillon shot himself in delirium; and hearing of the sad event, Cameron hurried back to see Murphy and learn particulars. At Kasekerah, where the suicide had happened, Cameron collected his men and started thence, accompanied by Bombay, on December 2, 1873.

It was not till the following February that Cameron and his party reached Tanganyika. Canoes had been sent hither for his use: and in them he was enabled to reach Ujiji, or rather Kowele, the landing-place.

By the last of April, the boats reached the end of the lake, and of the district near which Livingstone had passed in his last fatal march. The outlet of the lake was discovered, and the important fact revealed that the Lukuga carries its stream into the Lualaba, which had been discovered by Livingstone, who thought it belonged to the "Nile system;" while Cameron declared it was a branch of the Congo. The true solution of the problem was left for Stanley, as we shall see later.

The expedition left Kwakasongo on August 1, and after two marches came in sight of the mighty Lualaba —a strong, sweeping current, fully a mile wide, and flowing at the rate of three or four knots an hour, with many islands, like the eyots in the Thames, lying in its course. The crocodiles and hippopotami were numerous and dangerous. Without delay Cameron started for Nyangwé, and was carried at a rapid pace down stream. "At last," he says, "I was at Nyangwé, and now the question before me was, what success would attend the attempt at tracing the river to the sea."

In the beginning of August, 1875, the Zambesi was seen, and at the end of the month Katende, near Lake Dilolo, was reached. Livingstone had penetrated so far. Then the want of food began to make itself felt. The pleasant traders with whom Cameron journeyed had stripped him of nearly all he possessed, and he was actually obliged to sell his shirts for food. So the march proceeded. In November the Kukewi River was crossed; then they marched through the mountains,

THE ZAMBESI.

until the approach to Katombela, on the coast, filled Cameron with delight.

A messenger sent in advance had obtained provisions which reached the half-starved explorer, and when within sight of the sea, Cameron ran down the slope of the hill towards Katombela, "swinging his rifle round his head." Unfurling the English flag he carried, Cameron advanced, and met a Frenchman, who, with three men bearing wine, welcomed him, and drank to the health of the first European who had crossed the Continent from east to west, Livingstone having performed the same feat in a contrary direction.

After a delay caused by sickness, Cameron proceeded to Loanda. Here he found letters and a hearty welcome, and having seen his people off in a schooner for Zanzibar, in February, 1876, he embarked for Liverpool in the steamer *Congo*.

The results of this journey across Africa were very important. The traveler proved that the Lualaba has no connection with the Nile system, and was of opinion that it was the head-waters of the Congo, a result which Stanley has since ascertained to be true. Thus Livingstone was actually exploring the Congo, and not the Nile, during his later years. Cameron also discovered a water system by the Lomané, which he called the true Lualaba.

For his great services to geographical science, the gallant explorer received the Gold Medal of the Geographical Society, and it has seldom been more worthily bestowed. Cameron was not only a successful traveler, but he was an accomplished observer. His observations were conducted on scientific principles and were of vast extent, displaying untiring industry under the most depressing influences of climate, and constancy and courage of a high order.

CHAPTER XV.

Stanley's Exploration of the Congo.

Once again Stanley appears on the scene, commissioned jointly by the *Daily Telegraph* and the *New York Herald*, to complete the discoveries of Speke and Livingstone, especially to clear up all doubts regarding the Central African Lakes, and to follow the Lualaba until it reaches the sea, the task which Livingstone sought to accomplish. His party from England consisted of Frank and Edward Pocock, Frederick Barker, and Halleck. A barge named the *Lady Alice*, was taken in sections, besides two other boats, with a perfect equipment.

Stanley left England, to begin his perilous journey, on August 15, 1874. He reached Zanzibar on September 21, and left for the mainland on November 12, and five days later, started for the interior, on his perilous and famous journey through Africa, of which he has given so graphic an account in his work, "Across the Dark Continent."

The first stage was to the Victoria Nyanza, which Stanley desired to explore. The imperfect description of previous explorers had left much to be decided concerning this great inland sea.

The advance to the great Lake Victoria was full of adventurous interest. Those who read his volumes will learn that traveling in the " Dark Continent " means being at times in the wilderness without a guide, or with traitors acting as guides, which is a worse alternative. This was Stanley's fate, and he was deserted in the waste, with a small stock of food. Through the difficult jungle the men had to crawl, cutting their way, guided solely by the compass, overcome by hunger and thirst, with desertions frequent, and much sickness. This was in " famine-stricken Ugogo."

While on this disastrous march he lost five of his people, who, " wandering on helplessly, fell down and died." The country produced no food, or even game, unless lions could be so called. Two young lions were found in a den, and were quickly killed and eaten. Stanley tells us how he returned to camp, and was so struck by the pinched jaws of his followers that he nearly wept. He decided to utilize his precious medical stores, for the people were famishing. So he made a quantity of gruel, which kept the expedition alive for 48 hours, and then the men he had despatched to Suma for provisions, returned with food. Refreshed, they all marched on, so that they might reach Suma next morning.

After proceeding 20 miles they came to the cultivated districts and encamped. But the natives of Suma were hostile, and the increasing sick-list made a four days' halt necessary. There were 30 men ailing from various diseases. Edward Pocock was taken ill here, and on the fourth day, he became delirious; but the increasing suspicions of the natives—who are represented as a very fine race—made departure necessary, and so a start was made, on January 17, 1875, in hostile company. The famine in Ugogo had severely tried every man's consti-

THE CONGO KING.

tution, and all felt weary in spirit if not ill in body. "Weary, harassed, feeble creatures," they reached

Chiwyu, 400 miles from the sea, and camped near the crest of a hill 5400 feet high. Here Edward Pocock breathed his last.

Hence two rivulets ran, gradually converging and finally uniting into a stream which trends towards Lake Victoria. Up to this point the explorer had, as he said, "child's play" to what he afterwards encountered.

After passing Mangina the expedition pushed on and reached Izanjih, where Halleck was seized with asthma. He would lag behind, and so Stanley proceeded slowly to Vinyata, where the expedition arrived on January 21, 1875. Here a magic doctor paid Stanley a visit and cast longing eyes at the stores. Scouts had been meantime sent after the man Halleck, and he was found murdered on the edge of a wood, his body gashed by many wounds.

Next day, after the departure of the magic doctor, who came for another present, the natives showed hostile symptoms. One hundred savages, armed and in warlike costume, came around, shouting and brandishing their weapons. At this juncture Stanley, following Livingstone's practice, decided to make no counter demonstration; but to remain quiet in camp, and provoke no hostility. This plan did not answer, however. The natives mistook for cowardice the wish for peace. There were so many tempting articles and stores which the natives coveted. No peace could be made at any price, and the savages attacked the camp in force.

Stanley disposed his men behind hastily erected earthworks and other shelter, and used the sections of the *Lady Alice* barge as a citadel for final occupation. There were only 70 effective men to defend the camp, and these were divided into detachments and subdivided. One sub-detachment was quickly destroyed, and in the day's fight 21 soldiers and one messenger were killed —three wounded. Stanley's men, however, pursued the retreating enemy, and burned many villages, the men bringing in cattle and grain as spoils. Next day the natives came on again, but they were quickly routed, and the expedition, after three days of battle, continued its way through the now desolate valley unmolested.

The victors, however, had not much to boast of. After only three months' march, the expedition had lost 120 Africans and one European from the effects of sickness and battle. There were now only 194 men left. They pressed on, however, towards the Victoria Nyanza, and after escaping the warlike Mirambo, who fought everybody on principle, Stanley reached Kagehyg on February 27. He was now close to the lake, having marched 720 miles; average daily march, ten miles.

On March 8, Stanley, leaving Frank Pocock to command the camp, set forth with eleven men in the *Lady Alice* to explore the lake and ascertain whether it is one of a series, as Livingstone said it was. The explorer began by coasting Speke Gulf. Many interesting observations were made. He penetrated into each little bay and creek, finding indications that convinced him that the slave-trade is carried on there. But the explorer had to battle for his information. Near Chaga the natives came down, and after inducing him to land, attacked him; but Stanley shot and killed one man, and the natives subsided. On another occasion the natives tried to entrap him, but he escaped by firing on the savages, killing three men and sinking their canoes with bullets from an elephant rifle.

Continuing his course now unopposed, Stanley coasted along the Uganda shore, and a messenger came from the King to Stanley requesting his attendance. Five canoes escorted the travelers to Usavara, the capital of King Mtesa. The explorer landed on April 5, and was most kindly received, but closely questioned.

King Mtesa appeared almost a civilized monarch, quite a different being from what he had been when Speke and Grant visited him as a young man. He had become a Mohammedan, wore Arab dress, and conducted himself well. He entertained Stanley with reviews of canoes, a naval "demonstration" of eighty-four "ships" and 2500 men! Shooting-matches, parades, and many other civilized modes of entertainment were practised for the amusement of the white man. In Uganda the traveler was welcomed, and perfectly safe. Stanley met Bellfonds and Linant, whom Gordon had sent on a mission to Mtesa.

While exploring the lake, serious conflicts occurred at Bumbireh Island, where he had put in for food, but was not amicably received. After a time, however, he was induced to go ashore, and when he landed, the boat was immediately seized. The crew and Stanley rushed to the boat, while the crowd yelled and branished their weapons. Some presents checked the fury of the people; but their object was apparently to kill the white man. The chief, who had already stolen the oars, was anxious to secure Stanley's weapons, but he caused his boat to be suddenly pushed off. Furious with rage, they rushed to their canoes; but a few bullets and some elephant explosive shells settled the question. Of the savages, 14 were killed and two canoes sunk.

STANLEY'S EXPLORATION OF THE CONGO.

Paddling with the bottom-boards of the boat, Stanley's men pushed on through storm and rain, until a favorable wind at length carried the voyagers to camp. Here, on May 6, Frank Pocock met his chief, who then learned that Frederick Barker had died a fortnight before. This was sad news, and much trouble was still ahead of Stanley. Other men had died, and fever attacked the leader himself.

In the continuation of his voyage Stanley again came into collision with the people of Bumbireh. Finding they would not return his oars, he sailed with 18 canoes to chastise them in Bumbireh Island.

Here he was expected, and the fight begun. Stanley, by pretending to land, drew the enemy from their ambush, and then fired on them, killing 42 of them; and this put an end to the resistance of the tribe. Their treachery was sufficiently punished, and they had declined peace. Stanley then proceeded to the Court of Uganda, where he found Mtesa at war.

Stanley had now explored the entire coast of the Victoria Nyanza, and found only one outlet, the Ripon Falls. The King was at the head of a numerous army, which had some skirmishing. While the army was encamped, and making ready for its final advance, Stanley converted King Mtesa to Christianity.

After remaining some time with Mtesa, he departed in October, 1875, to explore the country lying between Muta Nzige (Albert Nyanza) and the Victoria Nyanza. This time he had with him an escort of Mtesa's men, under a "general" named Sambusi. The expedition, after a pleasant march, came within a few miles of the Albert Nyanza, but then the native warriors wished to return, and Stanley yielded perforce. He returned, but the faint-hearted "general" was put in irons by Mtesa, whom he had disgraced. Stanley had now confirmed Speke's discoveries. He proceeded towards the Alexandria Nile and thence turned towards Lake Tanganyika, and camped at Ujiji, where he had met Dr. Livingstone. Thence he prepared to journey to Nyangwé, the farthest northern place attained by Cameron, as already related. Stanley carried the *Lady Alice* across 350 miles which intervened between Ujiji and Nyangwé, which is situated on the Lualaba (of Livingstone), which Stanley demonstrated to be none other than the mighty Congo. We shall now follow Stanley briefly in his discovery along that river, which he had determined to explore.

On November 5 he set out from Nyangwé. He had with him 140 rifles and 70 spearmen and could defy the warlike tribes of which he had heard so much, and he made up his mind to "stick to the Lualaba, fair or foul!" For three weeks he pushed his away along the banks, meeting with tremendous difficulties, till all became disheartened. Stanley said he would try the river. The *Lady Alice* was put together and launched, and then the leader declared he would never quit it until he reached the sea. "All I ask," said he to his men, "is that you will follow me in the name of God." "In the name of God, master, we will follow you," they replied. And they did so bravely.

A skirmish occurred at the outset, by the Ruiki River, and then the Ukassa Rapids were reached. These were passed in safety, one portion of the expedition on the bank, the remainder in canoes. So the journey continued, but under very depressing circumstances, for the natives, when not openly hostile, left their villages, and would hold no communication with the strangers. Sickness was universal. Small-pox, dysentery, and other diseases raged, and every day a body or two was tossed into the river. A canoe was found, repaired, and constituted the hospital, and so was towed down stream. On December 8, a skirmish occurred, but speedily ended in the defeat of the savages, who had used poisoned arrows. Again, another serious fight ensued, the savages rushing against the stockades which surrounded the camp, and displaying great determination. The attack was resumed at night. At daybreak, a part of the native town was occupied, and there again the fighting continued. The village was held, but the natives were still determined, and again attacked; the arrows fell thickly, and it was a very critical time for the voyagers.

Fortunately the land division arrived and settled the matter. The savages disappeared, and the marching detachment united with Stanley's crews. That night Pocock was sent out to cut away the enemy's canoes, and the danger was over. But now the Arab escort, which had joined Stanley at Nyangwé, became rebellious, and infected the rest. Stanley feared that all his people would mutiny, but he managed them with a firm and friendly hand. All this time the people had been dying of fever, small-pox and poisoned arrows, and constant attacks of the enemy prevented burial of the dead or attendance of the sick and wounded.

On December 26, after a merry Christmas, considering the circumstances, the expedition embarked, 149 in all, not a man having deserted. On January 4, 1877, they reached the first of a series of cataracts, now named Stanley Falls. This was a cannibal country, and the man-eaters hunted the voyagers "like game." For 24 days the conflict continued, fighting, foot by foot, the 40 miles or so which were covered by the cataracts, and which the expedition had to follow by land, foraging, fighting, encamping, dragging the fleet of canoes, all the time with their lives in their hands, cutting their away alike through the forest and their deadly enemies.

Yet, as soon as he had avoided the cannibals on land, they came after him on the water. A flotilla of 54 canoes, some of great size, with a total of nearly 2000 warriors, were formidable obstacles in the way. But discipline and gunpowder won the day, and the natives were dispersed with great loss and the village plundered of its ivory. In effecting this great success Stanley only lost one man, making the sixteenth since the expedition had left Nyangwé.

Some of the cataracts Stanley describes as magnificent, the current boiling and leaping in waves six feet high. The width in places is 2000 feet, narrowing at the falls. After the great naval battle, Stanley found friendly tribes who informed him the river, the Lualaba, which he had named the Livingtone, was surely the Congo. Here was a great geographical problem settled. Proceeding on his way, Stanley encountered further determined opposition, but he overcame all resistance and pushed on rapidly. Soon the friendly tribes were again met with, and at length the warfare with man ceased, but the struggle with the Congo continued.

There are 57 cataracts and rapids in the course of the river from Nyangwé to the ocean, a distance of 1800 miles. One portion of 180 miles took the explorer five months. During that terrible passage, of which graphic details are given in his work, he lost

STANLEY FALLS.

many of his followers, including the brave Pocock and Kalulu—the black boy.

March 12 found them in a wide reach of the river, named Stanley Pool, and below that they "for the first time heard the low and sullen thunder of the Livingstone Falls." From this date the river was the chief enemy, and at the cataracts the stream flows like a mill-race. The canoes suffered or were lost in the "caldron," and *portages* became necessary. The men were hurt also; and Stanley had a fall, and was half-stunned. There were only 17 canoes remaining on March 27. The descent was made along shore below Rocky Island Falls, and in gaining the camping-place, Kalulu, in the *Crocodile* canoe, was lost. This boat got into midstream, and went gliding over the smooth, swift river to destruction. Nothing could save it or its occupants. It whirled round three or four times, plunged into the depths, and Kalulu and his canoe-mate were seen no more. Nine men, including others in other canoes, who were likewise swept over, were lost that day. By April 21 thirty-seven days had passed in covering 34 miles. One big fall only remained, the voyagers were told, and so they resolved to persevere till they had passed it; but subsequently, on May 17, a chief informed them that five falls were in front. Mowa was quitted on June 3, and a new camp was to be pitched above the great cataract, near Zinga. These falls proved to be whirlpools, and not rapids. Stanley went up to Zinga Point to survey the rapids, when he perceived a canoe tumbling about in the Massassa Pool. It was capsized, and he sent men to aid the wrecked with ropes in the little bay to which the current tended.

The men struggled to avoid the cataract, and impelled

the boat toward the land. They gained it nearly, then they swam ashore, while the current swept the canoe away into the whirlpools. Eight only of the occupants were saved. Three were lost and one was Pocock, "Little Master," as he was called. By some fatal rashness he had urged the coxswain, against his will, to try the stream, and though repeatedly told of the danger, he had persisted in urging the men to the attempt. He paid a heavy penalty for his rashness.

The descent by the river had cost Stanley, besides Pocock, and many of the natives, 1800 dollars' worth of ivory, 12 canoes, and a mutiny, not to mention grave anxiety and incessant cares and conflicts.

After a weary time, nearly starved, the remainder of the expedition, reduced to 115 persons, arrived at Boma, on August 9, 1877, nine months from the date they left Nyangwé. Stanley thus demonstrated that the Lualaba is the Congo, and opened up a splendid waterway into the interior of the "Dark Continent," which the African International Association—founded by the King of the Belgians, in 1876, for the suppression of the slave-trade and the civilization of the interior—has planted with stations over a wide extent of country.

At the request of the enlightened ruler of Belgium, Stanley undertook the task of organizing the administration of the Congo Free State, which received its first impulse from the great explorer, who returned to Africa in the following year to start the infant State on its course of progress and civilization. Under the rule of Stanley the Congo Free State became a pattern to the other Colonies of what such an administration should be, and, but for his untimely end, General Gordon would have carried on the grand work of civilization.

CHAPTER XVI.

Stanley's Rescue of Emin Pasha.

ONE of the results of the abandonment of the Soudan by the Egyptian Government was that Emin Pasha, governor* of the Equatorial Province, was placed in great jeopardy after the death of General Gordon at Khartoum, in January, 1885. A Relief Committee was formed in London, and a sum of $100,000 was subscribed, including $50,000 from the Egyptian Government, and $5,000 from the Geographical Society.

From accounts which leaked out of Emin Pasha's position, in which English people took a keen interest, as in great part due to the policy forced on the Khedive by the action of their Government, it seemed that he remained undisturbed till the beginning of 1874, when the Mahdi's followers invaded the Bahr-el-Ghazel Province, and carried off its governor, Lupton Bey. Emin,

---

* The other governors under General Gordon's orders as Governor-General of the Soudan, were Slatin Bey, in Kordofan, and Lupton Bey in the Bahr-el-Ghazel Province. Not long after Gordon's death, Slâtin surrendered his province to the Mahdi, and Lupton, being attacked, also yielded obedience, and became, like Slatin, an enslaved captive. Emin alone held out and defended himself successfully against all the efforts of the Mahdist generals, withdrawing from position to position, and stubbornly defending each in turn.

expecting that he would soon be assailed, withdrew all his troops and stores from Lado to Wadelai. In this remote corner of Central Africa, whence he was rescued

EMIN PASHA.

by Stanley, he was able to carry on his work unmolested. But discontent was brewing among his people, and supplies and ammunition were running short.

Emin wrote from Lado, November 16, 1884, imploring

Mr. Mackey, the English Missionary, to inform his correspondents that by their aid the Egyptian Government might learn his position, and help be sent to him, or, as he said, "we perish."

On January 1, 1886, he wrote, "Two years and a half are passed away since I had the last news from our Government. The Bahr-el-Ghazel Province (Lupton Bey's) has been overwhelmed by the followers of the false prophet, and with the greatest exertions only I have been able to preserve this province (the Equatorial) from a similar fate. I have lost a good many gallant men; we rest now a little flock in the midst of thousands of negroes. Our munitions are nearly exhausted, our people short of their most modest wants (clothing); our way to the north has now been cut off by Arabs and negroes. So I came here and opened intercourse with the King of Unyoro, who kindly assisted me, and I venture now to forward you some letters by way of Uganda and Unyanyembe, requesting you most earnestly to send the despatches for the Prime Minister in Cairo as soon as possible by way of your official post. The existence of our people may depend upon them."

Emin wrote in a similar strain to the Anti-Slavery Society. These letters appealed to the generous instincts of the English people, who, after the death of Gordon, and the fate of Lupton and Slatin, recognized in the Governor of the Equatorial Province the last of the lieutenants of their great and much regretted countryman. When suggestions for his relief began to take shape, Stanley was applied to, just as he was about to leave England for America on a lecturing tour. Asked, " Would you be willing to lead the Relief

Expedition?" he replied, "If your choice devolves on me, and you are really in earnest, I will accept the command instantly and gratuitously; but if the choice of the Committee devolves on Mr. Thompson, I will subscribe $2500 to the Relief Fund."

In a letter dated November 15, 1886, Stanley expresses his readiness to go at once, and states that he had been examining the question of routes, of which he said there were four from which to select. He was allowed to proceed to America, but on December 11, he was telegraphed, in the following terms: "Your plan and offer accepted. Authorities approve. Funds provided. Business urgent. Come promptly. Reply."

The answer came from New York; "Just received Monday's cablegram. Many thanks. Everything all right. Will sail per *Eider*. If good weather and barring accidents, arrive December 22, Southampton. It is only one month's delay, after all. Tell authorities prepare Holmwood, Zanzibar, and Seyyid Barghash." Thus the work of the rescue of Emin Pasha was fairly started.

Shortly after his arrival in England, Stanley paid a visit to the King of the Belgians, at Brussels, in whose service he was still retained. After mature consideration, the route by the Congo was chosen as the most desirable, and Stanley had reason to congratulate himself on the selection.

On this point of route, Stanley says that the simple reason why he adopted that by the Congo, was "to ensure success." When the expedition was committed to his charge, he decided instantly in favor of the Congo route. Both routes, by the east and west coasts, were familiar to him for nine-tenths of the distance, as he had penetrated to within 150 miles of Lake Albert from Zanzibar, and 320 miles from the side of the Congo. But the Emin Relief Committee expressed their preference for the route from the east coast, and preparations were at once set on foot with that object. Under orders sent to Zanzibar, several tons of rice were forwarded 200 miles inland, 60 baggage animals, and $2000 worth of saddlery were purchased, besides goods valued at $5000, and one steel boat was ordered.

The Congo route was adopted, not however, so completely but that a change might be effected any moment, if it were necessary, on arriving at Zanzibar. This change of route, had one mischievous effect. There was no time to order the construction of a steam flotilla, which would have carried the entire expedition up the Congo, to within 60 miles of the Albert Nyanza, and he had to be content with one boat only, and arrange that a rear column should follow with the remainder of the men and stores.

Meantime, Stanley was busy collecting supplies and selecting a staff of officers to accompany him. He received hundreds of applications from all parts. The task of making a selection was a difficult one, but the result has proved that the choice was judicious.

The following were selected—Major Edmund Barttelot, distinguished in Afghanistan and the Nile campaigns; Lieutenant W. G. Stairs, of the Royal Engineers, lately engaged on the survey in New Zealand; Captain R. H. Nelson, who had served in Zululand and against the Basutos; Surgeon T. H. Parke, Army Medical Department; A. M. Bonny, of the same service; John Rose Troup, Herbert Ward, an explorer in Borneo and New Zealand. Two gentlemen, Mounteney

Jephson and J. S. Jameson, having applied rather late, were admitted upon payment of $5000 each, which sums were added to the Relief Fund. Of these gentlemen, Major Barttelot and Mr. Jameson never returned.

Quitting England in January, 1887, Stanley arrived at Alexandria on the 27th, and, proceeding on to Cairo, had interviews there with the Khedive and Mr. Junker, who was returning after many years' absence in the Soudan and Equatorial Africa. Zanzibar was reached on February 21, and so well had everything been arranged, that, on the 25th, Stanley sailed from Zanzibar for the Congo by the Cape of Good Hope.

The *personnel* of the expedition

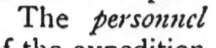
TIPPOO TIB.

consisted of 800 men. There were 11 English officers; 605 Zanzibari men and 12 Zanzibari boys; 62 Soudanese and 13 Soomaulis. In addition, there were embarked in the ship Tippoo Tib and 96 of his people. Some special mention is required of this remarkable Arab chief, who has played an important part in Central African explorations. While at Brussels, Stanley was consulted by the King of the Belgians respecting Tippoo Tib and the

Congo State. He advised that he should be employed as an agent of the Congo State, it being a far cheaper and more humane method to disarm his hostility than the costly method of force, and he was entrusted with the mission to negotiate with him. With the aid of the Consul at Zanzibar, Tippoo Tib was enlisted as the salaried governor of the Stanley Falls region, whose duty it would be to arrest the advance of the Arabs down the Congo and to save the stations on its banks from the devastation which, in 1883, had already commenced below the Falls. Stanley also obtained Tippoo's signature to a formal contract, that he would furnish him with a contingent of 600 Manyuema carriers, to be paid for at the rate of thirty dollars a head, to assist in th carriage of the goods and ammunition for Emin Pasha's force, for which promise he was given a free passage for himself and 96 of his followers from Zanzibar to Stanley Falls, and also free rations.

On March 24, 1887, the expedition began the overland march to Leopoldville, at Stanley Pool, 235 miles from Metadi, which was reached on April 21. Three days after Stanley mustered his force, when it was found that the number was already reduced by 63 men and 28 rifles out of 524. Three-fourths of this loss was due to desertion, which is characteristic of an expedition consisting of Zanzibaris. "It is a proof," he says, "if any were needed, of the disaster that would have overtaken us had we proceeded by any East African route on such a distant mission." Yet this was but the beginning of his troubles on this head. Desertion continued from the day he began the land march at Metadi, until he arrived within a few days' march of Zanzibar.

At Stanley Pool it was found that the steamers promised by the King of the Belgians were not ready, though, after undergoing some repairs, the *Stanley* was made available. There remained the steamer *Peace*, of the Baptist Mission, and the *Henry Reed*, of the Livingstone Mission. On the steamer *Peace*, and two boats, were embarked 112 people and their loads; the *Henry Reed* and two boats held 131 and their loads, and the steamer *Stanley*, with the hulk *Florida*, took up 364—total, 607. The flotilla steamed from Stanley Pool on May 1, and on the 12th arrived at Bolobo. The *Stanley* steamer was instantly despatched back again down stream for the remainder of the men who were marching along the south bank of the Congo from the Pool, and the expedition was assembled at Bolobo by May 14. Leaving 131 men at Bolobo, under Ward and Bonny, the flotilla resumed its journey up the river.

On June 16, after a voyage of 1050 miles from Stanley Pool, the flotilla made fast to the landing-place of Yambuya, on the Lower Aruwhimi, just below the first rapids, and without trouble or bloodshed occupied the village. Meantime the *Henry Reed* and lighters had been despatched to Stanley Falls with Tippoo Tib and his people, who had thus been saved a year's journey on foot.

When the flotilla parted, Tippoo Tib said that, nine days after arrival at his station, he would set out with his 600 carriers for Yambuya camp, to join Stanley in his march to the Albert Nyanza.

If Tippoo Tib arrived with his carriers, Major Barttelot was to march with his column and follow Stanley's track, which, as long as it traversed the forest region, would be known by the "blazing" of the trees and by the camps, but in the event of Tippoo Tib and his carriers not coming as promised, he was to proceed by double or treble stages until he should be met by the advance column, under Stanley, returning from the Albert Nyanza to relieve him.

On June 28, 1887, Stanley set out from Yambuya with the advance column, consisting of Captain Nelson, Lieutenant Stairs, Mr. Jephson and Dr. Parke, and 389 men, and set his face on his adventurous journey through the forest. The objective point was Kavalli, distant, in a direct line from Yambuya, 322 miles, and until it was traversed by the expedition, the region was entirely unexplored and untrodden by the foot of either white man or Arab. They bore with them a steel boat, twenty-eight feet by six feet, about three tons of ammunition, and two tons of provisions and sundries. Of the entire body of 389, some 180 were reserved men, half of whom were pioneers, carrying, besides their Winchester rifles, axes and bill-hooks to pierce the bush and cut down obstructions.

He entered the forest with confidence, but on emerging from its horrid shade, found that it extended in an unbroken wave, beginning at the confluence of the Congo with the Aruwhimi, and maintaining the same aspect, density and character, across nearly four and one-half degrees of longitude. Though daily expecting to hear from natives some news of a grassy country lying north, south, or east of them, it was not until they were seven days' march from the grassy region that they encountered any one who had ever heard of grass-land. To the rest all the world was overgrown with one endless forest.

For a few days after Stanley set out, news of him was received at the camp at Yambuya, and then, as he

THE ADVANCE THROUGH THE FOREST.

plunged deeper into the recesses of the African forest, all intelligence of his movements was lost to the world. Many months rolled by and no word came of the adventurous traveler. Rumors were rife of a great disaster, in which those who believed in the boundless resource and good luck of the remarkable man who had brought relief to Livingstone, placed no credit. Reports were prevalent in the Soudan and were brought to Suakin of a white Pasha whom some thought was Stanley, and he was represented as a successful warrior who had scattered the forces of the Mahdi and was marching on Khartoum. But all was conjecture and, as month succeeded month, the prospect of success, or even of Stanley's emerging alive from that wilderness, grew fainter.

The first definite news that arrived from the traveler was conveyed in a letter he had addressed to Tippoo Tib, dated, "Boma of Banalaya (Urenia), August 17, 1888," giving information of his safety and of having successfully performed his mission. This letter, which was brought by a messenger to Stanley Falls, reached Brussels on January 15, 1889. The remainder of the letters brought by this man remained at Stanley Falls, and did not arrive in Europe till the end of March.

And now we will follow Stanley's slow and painful steps on his journey to Emin Pasha at Wadelai, on the Albert Nyanza, and back again to the vicinity of his "good friend," or as he was to find him, his *faithless* ally, Tippoo Tib.

On June 28, the expedition quitted the camp at Yambuya, carrying 50,000 rounds of Remington ammunition and a ton of gunpowder as a first instalment of relief for Emin Pasha. They followed the riverbank, and at the end of a march of 12 miles arrived in the district of Yaukonde. Only the first five miles of this first day's march were tolerable, and then they had difficulties which impeded their movements and arrested progress for 160 days. These consisted of creepers varying from one-eighth of an inch to 15 inches in diameter, swinging across the path in " bow-lines," or loops, sometimes massed and twisted together, also of a low, dense bush, occupying the sites of old clearings, which had to be cut through before a passage was possible for the carriers, so that the pioneers with their axes and bill-hooks had no sinecures. During a great portion of each day the darkness was increased by the heavily-charged rain clouds.

The inhabitants of this forbidding region were in keeping with their sinister surroundings, being wild, savage and vindictive. The race of dwarfs called Wambutti were even worse. These pigmies were known to exist nine centuries before the Christian era. The geographer Hipparchus located these dwarfs near the Equator, close to the Mountains of the Moon, where Stanley discovered them twenty-three centuries later.

Stanley describes his first interview with this ancient and interesting race :—" Near a place called Avetiko, on the Ituri River, our hungry men found the first male and female of the pigmies squatted in the midst of a wild Eden, peeling plantains. You can imagine what a shock it was to the poor little creatures at finding themselves suddenly surrounded by gigantic Soudanese, six feet four inches in height, nearly double their own height and weight, and black as coal. But my Zanzibaris, always more tender-hearted than the Soudanese, prevented the clubbed rifles and cutlasses from extinguishing their lives there and then, and brought them to me as prizes. The height of the man was four feet; that of the woman a little less. He may have weighed about 85 pounds; the color of the body was that of a half-baked brick, and a light brown fell stood out very clearly. So far as natural intelligence was concerned, within his limited experience, he was certainly superior to any black man in our camp.

"We began to question him by gestures. 'Do you know where we can get bananas?'

"He grasps his leg to show us the size, and nods his head rapidly, informing us that he knows where to find bananas about the size of his leg.

"We point to the four quarters of the compass, questioningly. He points to the sunrise in reply.

"'Is it far?'

"He shows a hand's length. Ah, a good day's journey without loads, two days with loads.

"'Do you know the Iburu?' He nods his head rapidly.

"'How far is it?' He rests his right hand sideways on the elbow-joint.

"'Oh, four days' journey.'

"I suppose we must have passed through as many as 100 villages inhabited by the pigmies. Long, however, before we reached them they were deserted and utterly cleared out. Our foragers and scouts may have captured about 50 of these dwarfs, only one of whom reached the height of 54 inches. They varied from 39 to 50 inches generally.

"The agricultural settlements in this region are to be found every nine or ten miles apart, and near each settlement, at an hour's march distance, will be found from four to eight pigmy villages situated along the paths leading to it.

"The larger aborigines are very industrious, and form a clearing of 400 to 1000 acres. Amid the prostrate forest they plant their banana and plantain bulbs, and in 12 months the trees are almost hidden by the luxuriant fronds and abundant fruit of unrivaled quality, size and flavor. A forest village consists of from 20 to 100 families of pigmies, and probably in that area between the Iburu and Ituri Rivers there are as many as 2000 families living this nomadic and free life in the perpetual twilight of the great and umbrageous forest of Equatorial Africa."

On the first day of the journey in the forest they were attacked. The people set fire to their villages, and under cover of the smoke attacked the pioneers, when a skirmish ensued. The expedition had scarcely begun to traverse the inhospitable region between Yambuya and the grass-land within 50 miles of the Albert Nyanza, than they were initiated into the subtleties of savage warfare practised by the inhabitants, great and small alike. The path frequently had shallow pits, filled with sharpened splinters, or skewers, covered over with large leaves, which for barefooted people proved a terrible infliction. Often the skewers would perforate the feet quite through, in other cases the tops would be buried in the feet, causing gangrenous sores. In this manner the men were so lamed that few of them recovered to be of much further use.

On the second day they followed a path leading inland, but trending east, and for five days they continued on this road, through a dense population. On July 5, they diverged and struck the river again. As it was apparently free from rapids, Stanley launched the boat, as she not only carried the cripples, but also relieved the carriers of two tons.

From July 5, to October 18, they clung to the left bank of the Aruwhimi River. In favor of this course was the certainty of obtaining food, but its immense curves and long trend north-east caused Stanley, at times, to doubt the wisdom of so doing. The river retained "the width of from 500 to 900 yards, with an island here and there, the resort of oyster fishermen, whose calling was manifest by the piles of oyster shells"—one Stanley measured being 30 paces long, 12 feet wide at the base, and 4 feet high.

At almost every bend of the river was a village of conical huts, and in some of the bends were many villages, populated by some thousands of natives. After 17 days' continuous marching they halted for one day's rest, and, during the month of July, only four halts were made. They reached the Mariri Rapids on the 17th of that month, and those of Bandeya on the 25th. On August 1, the first death took place, but as they entered a wilderness, which occupied nine days to traverse, their sufferings increased, and several deaths occurred. Any attempts to deal with the natives for food by means of barter were useless. They would declare that they had none. Ultimately, Stanley and his men helped themselves to what they required in order to maintain life, and prepared food for the wilderness already referred to, where no food was procurable.

Above Panga the falls became more frequent. The character of the architecture, and of the language, had now changed. Below, the huts were of the "candle-

LIEUTENANT STAIRS WOUNDED BY A POISONED ARROW.

extinguisher" order; and, above the Rapids, the villages consisted of detached square huts, surrounded by tall logs, which formed separate courts. The walls of the huts are also screened with logs, precautions the natives are compelled to adopt against the poisoned arrows in use throughout the region.

At Avisibba, situated about midway between the Falls of Panga and the Nepoko, a tributary stream, the natives made a determined attack on a boatload of foragers. Five men were wounded with poisoned arrows, and also Lieut. Stairs. Fortunately the poison, in his case, was dry, having, in all probability, been put on some days before, and it was three weeks before he recovered his strength, though the wound was not closed for months. In the case of every wounded man death ensued from tetanus.

On revisiting this place, on their return march to relieve the rear column, Stanley discovered the nature of the poison. In the huts were several packets of dried red ants. These insects were ground into powder when in this state, and cooked in palm oil, when they were smeared over the wooden points of the arrows.

On August 15, Mr. Jephson, in command of the land party, led his men inland, and, losing his way, was not reunited with the main column until the 21st. Four days after, forming a junction, the expedition arrived opposite the mouth of the Nepoko. After a few days it was found that progress by the river became impossible. The canoes and steel boat were accordingly emptied of their loads, and the expedition started on the second stage of its journey, but famine, dysentery and ulcers had so sapped the strength of a great many of the men that they could, with difficulty, stagger along under their loads.

On August 21 the expedition encountered a party of Manyuema, belonging to the caravan of Ugarrowwa, or Uledi Balyuz, formerly a tent-boy of Speke, now become a wealthy and important personage. Up to this date Stanley had adopted the Congo route to avoid the Arabs, who he knew would tamper with his men and tempt them to desert. Within three days of this meeting no less than 26 men deserted. On September 16 they arrived at a camp opposite Ugarrowwa's station, but as food was very scarce, Stanley pushed on after a halt of only one day. All the Soomaulis, 51 in number, and five of the Soudanese, preferred to remain behind at this station, to the continuous marching, which would have been certain death to them owing to their state of health. Stanley arranged with Ugarrowwa to feed them, at five dollars a month for each man.

Between September 18 and October 18 the expedition was only able to traverse 50 miles of ground, to a settlement about 460 miles from Yambuya. It was the most terrible part of the journey, owing to the Arabs having so devastated the country that no food was procurable. They lived on fungi, a large bean-shaped nut, and wild fruit, and those who could not get sufficient perished or deserted the famine-stricken column to die elsewhere. Of the sufferings he and his followers had endured on this occasion Stanley says:—

" For six weeks they had not seen a bit of meat; for ten days they had not seen a banana or grain, and the faces of the people were getting leaner and their bodies were getting thinner, and their strength was fading day by day. One day the officers asked him if he had seen anything like it in any African expedition before. He replied, 'No,' though he remembered on a former occasion when they were nine days without food, and ended their famine with a fight. Then, however, they knew where there was grain, and all they had to do was to hurry on; but in the late expedition they had been ten days without food, and they did not know where their hunger was to terminate. They were all sitting down at the time, and he expressed his belief that the age of miracles was not altogether past. Moses struck water out of the Horeb rock, the Israelites were fed with manna in the wilderness, and he told them that he did not think they should be surprised to see some miracle for themselves—perhaps on the morrow or the following day. He had scarcely finished, when some guinea fowl flocked round them and were at once seized."

On October 18, they entered the settlement occupied by Kilonga-Longa. "No one," says Stanley, "white or black, belonging to the expedition, will ever forget that awful month." On leaving Ugarrowwa's station, the party numbered 273 souls, having left 56 there, and lost the balance by desertion and death. On reaching Ipoto, the Arab station of Kilonga-Longa, the column was still further reduced by the loss of 56 men from death or desertion.

To obtain food the starving men sold their ammunition, so that 3000 rounds were thus made away with. Over 30 rifles were also sold, and some of the people disposed of their clothes and equipments, and even entered the tents of the European officers by night and stole their bedding, which they disposed of to the slaves at the station. Surgeon Parke lost his entire kit of clothing; Captain Nelson had his blankets stolen, and Stanley lost his cutlery and spoons. The bonds of discipline were relaxed by the continuous suffering they had endured, and the people were thoroughly demoralized and jeered at their leaders. " It required," says Stanley, " an infinite patience to bear with their taunts and insolence. But their sufferings were great. They might have proceeded to extremities, and murdered the European officers who had beguiled them into this interminable forest only to die of starvation, and that they did not do so seems wonderful."

Stanley, finding that expostulations and mild punishments were of no avail, took two of the worst offenders, and hanged them in the presence of their comrades.

When the expedition issued from Kilonga-Longa's station to prosecute the march, the people were beggared, and some were almost naked. They had become so weakened by starvation that they were compelled to leave behind their boat, and about 70 loads of goods. In charge of these remained Surgeon Parke and Captain Nelson, who were unable to travel.

A march of 12 days, almost in a direct line, brought them to Ibwiri, within a few miles of which the Arab devastations had been carried. Between this point and Kilonga-Longa's station not a hut had been left standing, and what man had not laid waste, the elephants had destroyed, so that the whole region was a howling waste. But at Ibwiri they entered upon a region of plenty, supporting a large population.

Their sufferings from hunger, which began August 31, ended on November 12, by which date Stanley and his men were reduced to the condition of skeletons, and many of them were almost at the last gasp. Out of

389, which they numbered at the start from Yambuya, only 174 were left. In this land of plenty, where supplies were plentiful, a halt was made for the column to recuperate.

A relief party was sent back to bring on Captain Nelson and the sick men left at the station, which received the name of "Starvation Camp." This party was conducted by Jephson, of whom his leader says:

"The relief of Captain Nelson at Starvation Camp is a striking example of spirit, courage, and celerity of movement. Poor Nelson had been left in a most forlorn situation to await supplies of food for himself and 52 sick men who were unable to travel. For 18 days we had been unable to obtain carriers, but finally Jephson volunteered to return about 50 miles to convey food to the party. What had taken the wearied, suffering expedition twelve days he performed in two and a half days, and arrived when the party had been reduced to Nelson and five men. A few more days and not one would have lived to tell the tale. The enfeebled remnant was saved and brought safely, and left in the charge of Surgeon Parke."

Captain Nelson's position had been a truly desperate one, and he, like the other officers of the expedition, displayed great qualities. Stanley writes:

"No position was worse calculated to inspire courage and the virtue of endurance than the unhappy one which Captain Nelson was by force of adverse circumstances compelled to fill in October, 1887. There were 52 men most wofully smitten with disease of all kinds, and there was not a particle of provisions to be obtained in the neighborhood. The outlook was of the gloomiest kind. We left them with a promise that as soon as food could be procured we should send some to them. For 12 days the expedition labored on and searched one

FIRST SIGHT OF THE ALBERT NYANZA.

bank after another without success. Six of the most intelligent chiefs had been despatched in advance.

While these were wandering hopelessly bewildered by the apparently illimitable waste of woods, the expedition on the 12th day stumbled across an Arab settlement. Despite every effort, no relief party could be sent for nine days more and then, after 25 days' absence, Jephson found Nelson still in the camp with the dead, and only five left out of the 52. Those who had not died had fled or been lost.

"Hitherto," says Stanley, "our people were sceptical of what we told them, the suffering had been so awful, calamities so numerous, the forest so apparently endless, and they refused to believe that soon they should come to a land of grass, with cattle, and reach the Nyanza and Emin Pasha, whom they had come to rescue. They regarded it all as a pleasing tale, and the farther they were led into the recesses of the forest, the more hopeless appeared their condition." Stanley would say to them: "Cheer up, boys; beyond this lies a country where food is abundant, and where you will forget your miseries. Be men; press on a little faster." But they turned a deaf ear to his entreaties. Now, however, all was changed, and they regarded him with wonder as a superior being.

The expedition halted 13 days at Ibwiri, and revelled in fowls, goat's flesh, bananas, sweet potatoes and corn. The result was that when Stanley started, November 24, to make the 126 miles still intervening between this station and the Albert Nyanza Lake, the force was transformed from 173 skeletons—one had been killed by an arrow—to that number of strong, robust men, fit for any toil, and full of hope. On December 1 they sighted the open country from the top of a ridge connected with Mount Pisgah, so named from their first

VIEWING THE ALBERT NYANZA.

view of the Land of Promise beyond. A few more days' march, and on December 5 they emerged at length from the forest upon the plains.

When in England, Stanley thought he had made a liberal allowance when he set down a fortnight as the time that would be required for traversing this forest, but 160 days had elapsed while they made their painful and laborious way through that region of gloom and despair. That any member of the expedition should have issued alive out of this terrible forest, so destructive of life and depressing to the spirits, is marvelous, and no words can do justice to the buoyant courage of the leader of this forlorn hope of civilization, who never faltered, or lost faith, when success seemed hopeless.

But they had now issued from the Cimmerian darkness of the forest into the light of open day, with the blue vault of heaven overhead, and the rays of the blessed sun shedding warmth and happiness into their hearts. Stanley describes the scene: "Emerging from the forest, finally, we all became enraptured. Like a captive set free, we rejoiced at sight of the blue light of heaven, and freely bathed in the warm sunshine, and aches and gloomy thoughts were banished. We raced with our loads over a wide, unfenced field, and herds of buffalo, eland, and roan antelope, stood on either hand with pointed ears and wide eyes, wondering at the sudden wave of human beings, yelling with joy."

After a brief period of license, order was restored in the column, and the march was resumed. They entered the villages of the open country and regaled themselves on melons, plantains, bananas, and great pots full of wine. The fowls were chased, killed and cooked, and

THE PROMISED LAND: END OF THE GREAT CONGO FOREST REGION.

the goats were seized and decapitated. Every village was well stocked with provisions, and the men quickly regained their strength; and had spirit to undertake anything.

It was fortunate it was so, as they met with armed opposition from the inhabitants the whole way intervening between the forest and the Albert Lake. The region they were now about to traverse is inhabited by remnants of tribes who have migrated from Unyoro, Itoro, from the southward, and from other tribes to the northward.

The villages were scattered over a great extent of country so thickly that there was no other road except through them or the fields. From a long distance the natives had sighted the expedition, and prepared to stop their progress. "The war-cries were terrible; from hill to hill they were sent pealing across the valleys, the people gathered by hundreds from every point, and war-horns and drums announced that a struggle was about to take place. Such natives as became too bold were checked with but little effort, and a slight skirmish ended in the capture of a cow, the first beef tasted since we left the ocean. The night passed peacefully, both sides preparing for the morrow."

On December 10, Stanley attempted to open negotiations. The natives were anxious to know who they were, and the intruders were desirous to learn details of the people that barred the way. Hours were passed talking, both parties keeping a respectable distance apart. The parties said they were subject to Uganda, but that Kabba-Rega, the ruler of Unyoro, son of Mtesa, was their real King, Mazamboni holding the country for Kabba-Rega. They finally accepted cloth and brass rods to show Mazamboni, and his answer was to be given on the following day. In the meantime, all hostilities were suspended.

The morning of the 11th dawned, and they were told that it was Mazamboni's wish that they should be driven back from the land.

"Our hill," says Stanley, "stood between a lofty range of hills and a lower range. On one side of us was a narrow valley, about 250 yards wide, on the other side the valley was three miles wide. East and west of us the valley broadened into an extensive plain. The higher range of hill was lined with hundreds preparing to descend, and the broader valley was already mustering its hundreds. There was no time to lose. A body of 40 men was sent, under Lieutenant Stairs, to attack the broader valley, Jephson marched with 30 men east, and a choice body of sharpshooters was sent to test the courage of those descending the slope of the higher range. Stairs pressed on, crossed a deep and narrow river in the face of hundreds of natives, and assaulted the first village and took it. The sharpshooters drove the descending natives rapidly up the slope until it became a general fight. Meantime Jephson was not idle. He marched straight up the valley east, driving the people back and taking their villages as he went. By 3 P. M. there was not a native visible anywhere, except on one small hill about a mile and a half west of us. On the 12th we continued our march—during the day we had four little fights. On the 13th marched straight east, attacked by new forces every hour until noon, when we halted for refreshments.

"The Remington rifles of the column were too much for undisciplined valor. The 50 miles of intervening open country was now traversed, and 15 minutes after, Stanley cried out, 'Prepare yourselves for a sight of the Nyanza.'

"The men murmured and doubted, and said, 'Why does the master continually talk to us in this way? Nyanza, indeed! Is not this a plain and can we not see mountains at least four days' march ahead of us?'"

But, true enough, at midday the Albert Nyanza was below them. Now it was the turn of their leader to jibe at the doubters, but as he was about to ask them what they saw, "so many came to kiss my hand, and beg my pardon, that I could not say a word. This was my reward."

The mountains, they learned, were the mountains of Unyoro. Kavalli, the objective point of the expedition, was six miles distant as the crow flies. They stood at an altitude of 5200 feet above the sea, and 2900 feet below them glistened the waters of the southern end of the Albert Nyanza. Right across to the eastern side, every dent in its low, flat shores was visible, and, traced like a silver snake on a dark ground, was the tributary Semliki, flowing into the Albert from the south-west.

It was a memorable and proud moment in Stanley's life. After a short halt to enjoy the prospect, they commenced the rugged and stony descent, to gain the terrace that extends from the base of the plateau to the lake. Before the rear-guard had descended 100 feet, the natives of the plateau just left behind poured after them. Had they shown as much obstinacy on the plain as they now exhibited, the progress of the column might have been seriously delayed. The rear-guard was kept very busy until within a few hundred feet of the Nyanza plains.

That night they camped at the foot of the plateau wall. An attack was made on the camp, but the enemy were easily disposed of. Continuing their march in the morning, the column approached the village of Ka-Kongo, situate at the south-west corner of the Albert Lake. Three hours were fruitlessly spent attempting to make friends. The natives would neither exchange "blood-brotherhood" with the strangers, because they never heard of any good people coming from the west end of the lake, nor would they accept any presents. They were civil enough, but wanted to be left alone. The column was shown the path and followed it for a few miles, when they camped about half a mile from the lake.

From the natives of Ka-Kongo Stanley learned that there was no white man on the lake in the neighborhood; that no steamer had been seen since Mason Bey's, in 1877; that they had a faint rumor that there was a white man somewhere in Unyoro; and there might be another far to the north, but they knew nothing of him. Though it took Stanley three hours to extract this information from the villagers, after close questioning, it was found to be reliable. Emin Pasha, though established at Wadelai, on the north extremity of the lake, had never visited the south end of Albert Nyanza and up to this time had not even been heard of by the fishermen.

CHAPTER XVII.

STANLEY'S RESCUE OF EMIN PASHA (*Continued*).

DURING the next three days, Stanley discussed with his officers the information he had gleaned from the villagers, and arrived at the conclusion that his only course was to return to Kilonga-Longa's station for the boat, with which they could then navigate the Albert Nyanza and reach Emin Pasha at Wadelai. In order to store the extra goods, it would be necessary to build a fort, as the natives on the coast were aggressive.

The expedition retraced its steps from the lake on December 17, and, after some skirmishing with the natives, recrossed the Ituri, and, entering the forest region on January 8, 1888, arrived on the site selected in the extensive clearing of Ibwiri, eleven marches from the lake. Here they erected a fort, surrounded by a ditch, to which they gave the name of Fort Bodo, or "Peace," and having cleared the bush, planted about seven acres with corn, beans and tobacco. Stanley's first step was to send a party back to the Arab settlement of Kilonga-Longa, a distance of 80 miles, for the boat, and to escort Captain Nelson and Dr. Parke, with the invalids left at that place. Lieutenant Stairs, in command of the party, was instructed to be conciliatory towards the Arabs, as intemperate language, or even a haughty demeanor, might bring on a collision. Within 25 days, Lieutenant Stairs marched 160 miles, relieved Parke and Nelson, brought the boat, and returned, "having," says Stanley, "endeared himself to his followers, and made the Arabs respect him so highly as to yield to him in all he wished." Out of 38 sick in charge of these officers, only 21 were brought to the fort, the rest having died or deserted.

Two days later, Stanley again sent Stairs a distance of 184 miles to escort the 56 convalescents from Ugarrowwa's station to Fort Bodo. He returned to Fort Bodo after 69 days' absence, escorted couriers, with letters, to Major Barttelot, brought back the convalescents, in going and returning having marched by different routes.

On the day of this officer's departure, Stanley fell ill of a stomach complaint, called "sub-acute gastritis," and also suffered from a painful abscess on the left arm. Between February 18 and March 26 his life was in imminent peril. He could not partake of food, and was too weak to do anything for himself. Throughout his illness, Dr. Parke* nursed him with constant care and great skill.

Parke mentions how, when Stanley was apparently at the point of death, he said:—"Doctor, put up the Stars and Stripes and cheer me with something bright to look at, that I may at least die under the American flag."

On applying for the appointment of medical officer Dr. Parke wrote out with his own hand the terms of his engagement, of which one was "loyal and devoted

---

* Stanley's original intention was to dispense with a qualified medical officer, and it was well for him that Dr. Parke volunteered his services, and that they were accepted.

service " gratuitously. His leader has acknowledged with gratitude the noble way in which he fulfilled to the letter and the spirit this labor of love, and how throughout the expedition he worked unremittingly, and with singular skill to cure his patients, who varied from twenty to fifty daily, and at one time numbered 124, fully one-third of the total strength of the column.

It was not until April 2, 1888, that Stanley had sufficiently recovered to be moved in a hammock. The boat had been received, but Stairs had not returned with the convalescents, and Stanley resolved to wait no longer for him, but return to the Albert Lake. The party, headed by their leader in a hammock, and carrying the boat, set out from Fort Bodo, where Captain Nelson remained as commandant, Jephson and Dr. Parke accompanying Stanley.

The natives, who had sought to destroy them when first marching through their country, responded to Stanley's advances, and entered into an agreement to supply him with stores gratuitously and to wage war on the common enemy, the Wanyoro. Each day the natives brought gifts of plaintains, corn, goats and cattle, for which they would take no payment, and the wants of the expedition were supplied, while they furnished guides and carried their ammunition and goods.

One day's march from the lake, a chief handed Stanley letters from Emin, who, two months after their first arrival at the lake, had heard of the visit.

The boat was launched on the Nyanza, and Jephson left with a picked crew to communicate with the Pasha. On the second day, Jephson came to Mswa Station, the southernmost in the Equatorial Province, and May 1, Stanley and his men had the satisfaction of seeing the

THOMAS H. PARKE AND HIS FAITHFUL PIGMY.

steamer *Khedive* on the lake, and soon they welcomed in their camp at Nyamsassi, Emin Pasha, for whom they had gone through so much suffering, and his companion, Captain Casati, and a number of Egyptian officials. But now came the disillusionment. Instead of finding, as they anticipated, and as would be gathered by a perusal of his letters, a man eager to return to civilization from fulfilling an impossible task, they saw before them one who seemed content with his position, and only asked for ammunition and stores. Stanley says:

"Contrary to our expectations, we did not find the Pasha disposed to return to the sea, neither was Captain Casati; nor did any one impress us with his eagerness to return to civilization. They all seemed content to remain in the land. They praised it highly for its fertility and agreeable climate, they loved the natives, and praised everything connected with life in that region. All the Pasha and Casati seemed to care for was means of defence against occasional disturbances. None seemed to reflect that after our experiences of the forest few would care to repeat them; that the powerful Kings of Uganda and Unyoro would always be a bar to sure communication with the east coast; that caravans would never venture by Masailand to be decimated by famine and thirst for the uncertain profits to be derived from the dangerous risks of the journey; that no body of philanthropists would repeat these expensive outlays on behalf of a province so remote from the sea as Emin Pasha's, when there were thousands of square miles of equally fertile soil lying close to the ocean."

The united party stayed together until May 25, 1888, and then Stanley, who had been expecting the arrival of the rear column, under Major Barttelot, or at least some news of it, determined to return to Fort Bodo, and if no information had been received there, then to march back through the dreary forest region until he met his friend or heard news of him, dead or alive.

Leaving Jephson with Emin Pasha, and also a few Soudanese, Stanley started with the rest of his force for Fort Bodo, where they arrived early in June. Still there was no news of the rear column, and the anxiety of all daily deepened. Food was prepared in abundance to enable them to cross the dreaded wilderness in which they had all so nearly perished, and June 15 Stanley set out on his search for Major Barttelot's column, leaving Stairs in command at Fort Bodo, with Nelson and Parke, and 59 men as a garrison.

The column, he says, who now marched with him were very different from the weak, starving wretches who had on a former occasion entered the stations of Kilonga-Longa and Ugarrowwa. Then they were so dispirited by want that they had no pluck to resent the ill-treatment received at the hands of these chiefs and their men. But now, that they knew the country from Yambuya to the Albert, that they had witnessed the worst horrors of the wilderness, and had measured their strength against tribes from the presence of whom the slaves of Ugarrowwa and Kilonga-Longa would have fled, inspired them with the belief that in every way they were superior men to those for whose smile they had a few months before fawned. When the column entered Kilonga-Longa settlement, their bearing attracted attention, and though no one uttered a threat, Kilonga-Longa, of his own accord, collected what Remingtons there were with him and quietly laid them at Stanley's feet, pleading that it was the fault of his slaves and their ignorance, and that he would not bear malice. As he had no commission to punish any subjects of the Sultan of Zanzibar, Stanley coldly accepted the guns and assured him that he did not pretend to judge of his conduct, and would therefore leave the matter in the hands of his master.

Twenty-eight days' march from Fort Bodo brought them once more to Ugarrowwa's station. But it was now abandoned, the slave-trader and his hundreds of desperadoes having started home with 600 tusks of ivory.

"People in England," writes Stanley, "have not the slightest idea what the present fashion of ivory collecting, as adopted by the Arabs and Zanzibari half-castes west of the lake regions, means. Slave-trading becomes innocence when compared with ivory-trading. The latter has become literally a most bloody business. Bands consisting of from 300 to 600 Manyuema, armed with Enfield carbines and officered by Zanzibari Arabs, range over the immense forest-land east of the Upper Congo, destroying every district they discover, and driving such natives as escape the sudden fusillades into the deepest recess of the forest. In the middle of a vast circle described by several days' march in every direction, the ivory-raiders select a locality wherein plaintains are abundant, prepare a few acres for rice, and, while the crop is growing, sally out by twenties or forties to destroy every village within the circle and to hunt up the miserable natives who had escaped their first secret and sudden onslaughts.

"They are aware that the forest is a hungry wilderness outside the plantain grove of the clearing, and that to sustain life the women must forage far and near

THE KING OF THE IVORY COAST.

for berries, wild fruit and fungi. These scattered bands of ivory-hunters find these women and children an easy prey. The explosion of heavy-loaded guns in the deep woods paralyze the timid creatures, and before they recover from their deadly fright, they are rushed upon and secured. By the possession of these captives they impose upon the tribal communities the necessity of surrendering every article of value, ivory, or goats, to gain the liberty of their relatives.

"The ivory tusks that Ugarrowwa was bearing now to the coast had been acquired by just such destruction of human life, and condemnation to misery of the unhappy survivors of the tribal communities. What Ugarrowwa had within his elected circle, Kilonga-Longa performed with no less completeness, and with greater disregard to interests of humanity, within his reserve; and the same cruel, murderous policy was being pursued with dozens of other circles into which the region as far south as Uregga, north to the Welle, east to longitude 29° 30′, and west to the Congo, was parcelled out."

Early in August the column overtook the immense caravan of Ugarrowwa, his flotilla of 57 canoes laden with helpless children, girls, and young women. His hoard of ivory, equal to about fifteen tons, was at the landing-place of a village near Wasp Rapids, on the Ituri River.

With Ugarrowwa were found the surviving couriers who had been despatched from Fort Bodo, February 16, in search of Major Barttelot's column, and the mail, delivered to Ugarrowwa for transmission to the Major, on September 18, 1887, was also returned. The couriers had been specially unfortunate. Three of their number had been killed, and only five were whole from grievous arrow-wounds. Ugarrowwa's band of 40 picked men had been also unable to proceed below Wasp Rapids.

Pursuing their course down stream, on August 17, they discovered all that were left of the rear column within a palisaded village formerly belonging to the Banalya tribe, a few marches from Yambuya. Major Barttelot had been shot by one of his Manyuema headmen a year earlier; and Jameson had returned to Stanley Falls to secure from Tippoo Tib an Arab assistant to govern the unruly mob of Manyuema carriers, whom Tippoo Tib had, after eleven months' constant solicitations on the part of these officers, finally furnished with an inefficient leader. Troup had been invalided home in the previous May. Ward was somewhere on the Lower Congo, having been despatched, after nine months' stay at Yambuya, to cable to the Home Relief Committee some unauthenticated rumors respecting misfortunes which were said to have overtaken the advance column, and to ask for instructions.

Of the gallant band of officers, only Bonny* remained, and from him Stanley heard a sad tale of disaster and failure. He learned that on his arrival at Banalya Jameson died. It seems that on August 12 he commenced the descent of the Congo from Stanley Falls in a canoe, and that, five days later, he died of fever. Stanley witnessed in that crowded village some of the miseries they had endured. The small-pox was raging, six bodies lay unburied; and if any member of the

---

* Stanley expressly exempts Mr. Bonny from any blame for the misfortunes which overtook the rear column. On the day of the murder of Major Barttelot, when the property of the expedition was looted, Bonny recovered 300 loads, and by his firmness kept the remnant of the column intact until Stanley arrived.

rear column presented himself to his old comrades for recognition, they saw only a living skeleton.

Thus a well-equipped and organized column of 271 had been reduced to 102 miserable, starved wretches, and, in a great measure, this sad result was due to breach of contract on the part of Tippoo Tib, who induced Major Barttelot, by repeated promises to supply the carriers, which he had no intention of fulfilling, to delay his march in the track of the advance column. Not until eleven months after they were promised did the porters arrive, but in the meantime, the rear column, consisting of Zanzibaris and Soudanese, had lost three-fourths of their number in the camp from disease, caused in a measure by this long inaction.

Stanley now busied himself in reorganizing the expedition, and on August 31, 1888, began his return march to the Albert Nyanza, taking with him the surviving members of the rear column, including Mr. Bonny, and such Manyuema carriers as volunteered to accompany him. The goods and sick men were placed in a number of canoes he had collected.

The expedition experienced much opposition from the wild tribes, and some of the best men were killed. On October 30, four days' journey above Ugarrowwa's station, or about 300 miles from Banalya, Stanley abandoned his canoes and began his march along the north bank of the Ituri River. Two days later, they discovered a plantation of plantains in charge of the dwarf natives, when the people revelled in this luxury, and carried off a week's provisions of plantain flour. Ten days' march brought them to another plantation. During this time the small-pox made great ravages among the Manyuema carriers, but the Zanzibari men

ARRIVAL OF STANLEY WITH THE REAR COLUMN.

escaped, owing to their having been vaccinated on board ship.

Continuing along the right bank of the Ihuru, a tributary of the Ituri, about 60 yards wide, until they could find a crossing, they stumbled across a large village, called Andikuma, surrounded by a fine plantation of plantains, where the people, after many days' fast, gorged themselves with this food to such excess, that a large number were unfit for duty. A six days' march brought them to another flourishing settlement, called Indeman. They found a place where they could build a bridge to cross the river. Bonny and the Zanzibaris worked with such celerity, that in a few hours the Dui, as the right branch of the Ihuru River is called, was passed, and they crossed from the Indeman district into one entirely free from the ravages of the Manyuema. In this land, between the right and left branches of the Ihuru, the dwarfs, called the Wambutti, were very numerous, and came into constant collision with the rear-guard of the expedition.

Following elephant and game tracks in the required south-easterly direction, on December 9, they were compelled to halt to search for food in the middle of a vast forest. Stanley sent 150 armed men back to a settlement, 15 miles distant, on the route they had traversed, and many of the Manyuema carriers followed them to assist in foraging.

At this place the expedition was nearly overwhelmed with disaster, as is shown by the following extracts from Mr. Stanley's diary, written on December 14, six days after the departure of the foragers: "Six days have transpired since our foragers left us. For the first four days time passed rapidly—I might say almost pleasantly—being occupied in recalculating all my observations from Ugarrowwa to Lake Albert and down to date, owing to a few discrepancies here and there, which my second and third visits, and duplicate and triplicate observations, enabled me to correct. My occupation then ended, I was left to wonder why the large band of foragers did not return. The fifth day, having distributed all the stock of flour in camp, and killed the only goat we possessed, I was compelled to open the officers' provision boxes and take a pound pot of butter, with two cupfuls of my flour to make an imitation gruel, there being nothing else save tea, coffee, sugar, and a pot of sago in the boxes. In the afternoon a boy died, and the condition of a majority of the rest was most disheartening; some could not stand, but fell down in the effort. These constant sights acted on my nerves, until I began to feel not only moral, but physical sympathy as well, as though weakness was contagious. Before night a Madi carrier died; the last of our Soomaulis gave signs of collapse; the few Soudanese with us were scarcely able to move."

On the morning of the sixth day, the broth was made as usual, consisting of a pot of butter, a tin of condensed milk, and a cupful of flour, with water, for one hundred and thirty people. The case had now become desperate, and Stanley called Bonny and the leaders into council. Bonny offered to stay in camp if ten days' food was provided, while Mr. Stanley proceeded in search of the missing party. Accordingly a store of butter, milk, flour and biscuits was handed over to him.

On the afternoon of the seventh day, Stanley mustered all of his men, and addressing the 43 feeble, starving people who were to be left behind, informed them that he hoped to meet the foragers on the road and return rapidly with the food they had doubtless found, and encouraged them to keep up their hearts, though his own was heavy with anxiety and foreboding.

That afternoon Stanley traveled back nine miles, having passed several dead bodies on the road, and early on the following day, being the eighth on which the foragers had quitted the camp, he met them marching at their ease. He changed the pace into a quick-step, and within 26 hours of leaving Starvation Camp, they were back, bringing an abundance with them, and soon gruel and porridge were boiling, plantains were roasting and meat simmering in pots for soup.

"This," writes Stanley, "has been the nearest approach to absolute starvation in all my African experience. Twenty-one persons altogether succumbed in this dreadful camp."

Proceeding on their march on December 17, the Ihuru River was crossed on the following day, and Stanley pushed on for Fort Bodo with the greatest despatch. Marching through the forest, regardless of paths, they had the good fortune to strike the western angle of the Fort Bodo plantations on the 20th, which was two days before the expiration of the term of his absence, as arranged by Stanley seven months before. But here again, as in the case of the rear-guard, he was doomed to experience a disappointment. When leaving Jephson and Emin Pasha, they had both promised to be at Fort Bodo by the middle of August, or thereabouts, when it was arranged that the fort was to be evacuated and a new station formed near Kavalli, on the south-western side of Albert Nyanza. But Lieut. Stairs, who was still at Fort Bodo, with 51 out of his original

EN ROUTE TO THE COAST.

garrison of 59, had heard no word from Emin or Jephson since Stanley's departure. This filled the leader with anxiety on Jephson's account, for, as to Emin, he was convinced that he loved the country and his people, and the life he had led, too much to be induced to retire with him to the coast, and Casati, he considered, held the same views.

On December 23, having first set fire to the fort, which had so long sheltered the sick and feeble members of the expedition, Stanley started once more for the Albert Lake. In order to remove all the surplus stores left in the fort, some 50 loads, and those brought with the rear column, they had to work by relays, and double marches were made from Fort Bodo to the edge of the grass-land, in order to leave nothing behind that might be of service to Emin Pasha. On January 9, 1889, they reached the Ituri Ferry, which was the last halt in the forest region before reaching the open country; and selecting a good camping site, on the east bank of the river, Stanley left Lieut. Stairs in command with 124 people, including Nelson and Parke, and, two days later, continued his march for the Albert Nyanza.

They were welcomed by the people of the plains, who, fearing a repetition of the fighting in December, 1887, flocked to the camp headed by their chiefs, and tendered their submission, agreeing to supply contributions of grain and plantains, and bringing small droves of cattle for the subsistence of the strangers. They also constructed the huts for the camps, and brought fuel and water each day. On January 16, 1889, a messenger arrived from the friendly chief at Kavalli, with a packet of letters, one from Jephson, written at intervals of several days, and two from Emin, confirming Jephson's news. With amazement, Stanley read his lieutenant's letter, which was dated, "Dufflé, November 7, 1888," in which he stated that, on August 18, a rebellion broke out there, got up by some Egyptian officers and officials, and he and Emin were arrested and placed in confinement, though they feared to do any personal injury to the Pasha, who was popular with the soldiers.

Plans were also made to entrap Stanley on his return, and strip the expedition of its stores and supplies.

Emin Pasha confirmed this intelligence in his letter, but gave no hint of the course he proposed to adopt.

Stanley wrote a formal letter, which might be read by any person, and on a separate piece of paper, a postscript for Jephson's perusal. In this, addressed from Kavalli, on January 18, 1889, he says he is sending 30 of his own men and three of Kavalli's to the lake with his letters, and that he (Jephson) would be escorted to his camp, and added, that he must "be wise, be quick, and waste no hour of time."

On February 6, Jephson arrived at the camp at Kavalli, on the plateau above the lake, and, in a few words, he enlightened Stanley as to the views of Emin, and his friend Casati. "Sentiment," he said, "is the Pasha's worst enemy; no one keeps Emin Pasha back, but Emin Pasha himself." This expressed a correct estimate of Emin's character formed by Jephson, after an acquaintance lasting from May 25, 1888, to February 6, 1889.

Casati had no views on this question but those of the Pasha, with whose fortunes his own were bound up.

Stanley, in order to bring matters to a crisis one

way or the other, wrote to Emin urging him, in the strongest terms, to come to a decision; and on February 13, he received a letter from the Pasha, informing him that, on the preceding day, he had arrived with his two steamers "carrying a first lot of people desirous to leave this country under your escort," and adding, "as soon as I have arranged for cover for my people, the steamers have to start for Mswa Station, to bring on another lot of people waiting transport." Stanley sent carriers and an escort down to the lake, and on February 17, Emin Pasha arrived in his camp with about 65 people, also Selim Bey, and seven other officers, the deputation sent by the mutineers of the Equatorial Province. Emin was in *mufti*, but the officers, three of whom were Egyptians, and the remainder Nubians, of soldierly appearance, were in uniform.

To sum up Stanley's labors to this point, for the third time he had come to the Albert Nyanza from the west.

A wonderful record is the story of his marches. The first journey from Yambuya to the lake, 171 days; the second journey from the lake to Fort Bodo, 22 days; the third journey from the fort to the lake, 20 days; the fourth journey from the lake to Banalya, 82 days; and then this fifth journey from Banalya back to the lake, 107 days, making a total of 402 days.

Thus it is seen how for more than thirteen months out of a year and a half the leader was on the constant move, making his way through virgin forests that had neither road nor track; forcing his path through tangled brushwood and over rushing torrents;

MEETING OF STANLEY AND EMIN PASHA.

carrying in his train many thousands of pounds' weight of goods, provisions, and ammunition; harassed over and over again by warlike and suspicious savages; uncertain as to the means of providing food for his hundreds of followers; exposed to an unhealthy atmosphere, and personally suffering the pangs of hunger and privation. Such was the man who, in spite of climate, in spite of hostilities, in spite of famine, in spite of sickness, never swerved from his line of duty and devotion, but faced all difficulties, resolved to overcome them till his work was done.

Next day Lieut. Stairs arrived, with his column, from the Ituri River, and the same day, the durbar was held, the Pasha acting as interpreter between Stanley and the deputation, who presented him with a document, signed by the leaders in the province, regretting their action in deposing the Pasha, expressing loyalty to the Khedive, and a hope that he would allow a reasonable time for the officers to collect the troops and their families, and bring them to his camp. Learning from the Pasha that twenty days would be considered a reasonable time, Stanley consented, and sent them back with a written promise to this effect, but the Pasha was to remain meanwhile in his camp. The two steamers were employed bringing fresh batches of refugees to the camp on the plateau, 2800 feet above the Nyanza, with their loads, no less than 1355 in number; but the soldiers made no appearance.

Stanley waited until March 16, but there was no sign of the arrival of the troops, who numbered 1500 regulars, with 3000 irregulars and their families. At Emin's request the time was extended to April 10, and, meantime, there were frequent communications between the Egyptians in his camp and their compatriots at Wadelai. While Stanley was rendered uneasy by furtive meetings in his camp, the Pasha continued to express unbounded confidence in the loyalty of his men. On April 5, an attempt was made to steal several of the Remington rifles, and during the night Stanley received notice of the result of a secret meeting of the rebels in his camp. Accordingly, he mustered the fugitives, and gave them to understand that the death penalty would be inflicted on any one engaged in seditious plots.

On April 10, 1889, the Egyptians and their families and following, numbering 570 persons, escorted by the expedition and 350 carriers of the district, started for the south end of the Albert Nyanza on their journey towards Zanzibar. But their advance was arrested on the second day by an unexpected incident. Stanley was seized with a recurrence of his malady; his life was despaired of, and it was only by the care and skill of Surgeon Parke that, on May 8, he had sufficiently recovered to enable him to order the march for the coast.

Meantime the rebels continued their schemings. Rifles, equipment and ammunition were stolen every day. Parties of four or five deserted, and finally, twenty men disappeared with five rifles. Under Stanley's directions, a party of his men—of whom everyone of the 350 under his command were loyal to the core to him—was despatched in pursuit, and a ringleader and twelve men were discovered and brought back to the camp. Some letters, intended for the rebels at Wadelai, fell by accident into his hands, and in one of them, an Egyptian captain wrote to Selim Bey, at Wadelai, in the following terms:—"For God's sake, hurry up 50 soldiers to our aid. With their help, we may at least delay the march of the expedition until you arrive with your force. Had we 200, we could effect immediately what we mutually wish." This was plain-speaking enough, and by means of this, and other letters, Stanley became acquainted with the names of the traitors and their plans. Even Emin could no longer doubt their treachery, or their intention of carrying into effect the grand idea of effecting the "capture of the expedition, with all its members, arms, and property, and present it to the Khalifa, at Khartoum."

Stanley convened a court, consisting of the European officers in camp, by whom the ringleader, referred to above, was tried, found guilty, and sentenced to death. Stanley says: "The scene of the execution was most solemn, and it is my opinion that it affected the rebellious most profoundly, for during all their service in the Equatorial Province, not one death sentence was passed. They seemed to perceive that now there was another *régime*, and to understand that to play at revolt and mutiny was dangerous. We may observe the effect of the lesson taught, in the absolute peacefulness of the march hence to Zanzibar." The last Stanley heard of Selim Bey was on May 8, when he received a letter, taking him to task for compelling Egyptian officers to carry loads (which was an unfounded charge), and he ended by begging him to extend the time of his departure, and announced that some of the rebel officers and their adherents had broken into the storehouses and stolen the reserve ammunition and stores. Stanley replied that he would proceed forward at a slow rate, but could no longer delay his march.

But the attention of the leader of this great exodus was now fully taken up with measures for the security of the mixed mass of human beings under his charge. The route he adopted skirted the Baregga Mountains, at a distance of about forty miles from the Albert Nyanza. On the fourth day they arrived at the southern end of these mountains, when they became aware that Kabba-Rega, King of Unyoro, whose territories they now entered, intended to dispute their passage. But without making a great *detour* through the forest, which would have been fatal to most of the Egyptians, they had no option but to press on through the open grassland between it and the Semliki River.

On the first day of entering the Unyoro territory, they were attacked by the Warasura, or Wanyoro soldiers, many of whom had breech-loaders—Remingtons, Sniders, and Winchesters—who were beaten back. The effect of this defeat was to clear the country of the Warasura as far as the Semliki, though a second attack, with a like result, was made as they were ferrying across that river.

After crossing to the eastern shore of the Semliki, they entered the Awamba region, and for several days, marched through plantations of plantains in the clearings. Day by day, as they advanced, was brought into greater prominence a splendid range of snow-clad mountains, whose north-western base line they skirted, having an altitude of 18,000 to 19,000 feet above sea-level, which had first arrested their attention on arriving at the Albert Nyanza in May of the preceding year. This range, whence issue the streams which supply the Semliki, is called Ruwenzori, or the "Snowy Range," and might well be the "Mountains of the Moon" of the ancients, the fabled source of the Nile.

Stanley wrote to the Geographical Society of his discovery of this range of mountains, and of the lake, to which he gave the name of Albert Edward Nyanza. "Baker, in 1864, reported the Albert Nyanza to stretch 'illimitably' in a south-westerly direction from Vacovia; and Gessi Pasha, who first circumnavigated that lake, and Mason Bey, who, in 1877, made a more careful investigation of it, never hinted at the existence of a snowy mountain in that neighborhood, nor did the two last travelers pay any attention to the Semliki River. I might even add that Emin Pasha, for years resident at or near the Lake Albert, or Captain Casati, who, for some months resided in Unyoro, never heard of any snowy mountain being in that region, therefore we may well call it an unsuspected part of Africa. Surely, it was none of our purpose to discover it. It simply thrust itself direct in our homeward route and as it insisted on our following its base-line, we viewed it from all sides but the north-east."

The beginning of the Semliki Valley, extending from the Albert Lake in a south-west direction, is very level; for a distance of 30 miles it only attains an altitude of 50 feet above the lake. Beyond this is a region of dense and rank tropical forest, and the valley rises sensibly higher until, at about 75 miles from the Albert Nyanza, it has attained an elevation of about 900 feet above its waters. Here the forest region abruptly ends, and gives place to a stretch of grass-land until the Albert Edward Nyanza is reached.

Rounding the south-western extremity of Ruwenzori, two days later they entered Usongora, and camped on

RUWENZORI—THE SNOW MOUNTAINS.
(*Mountains of the Moon.*)

the shores of the newly-discovered lake, "which," says Stanley in his official report, "is, in reality, the source of the south-western branch of the White Nile."

Pushing on, they skirted Ruanda, an extensive country lying between this river and the Congo watershed to the west, and now entered the better-known land of Karagwé, south of that river, on the shores of the Victoria Nyanza. They were welcomed by the grateful people as their deliverers from the dreaded Wanyoro, and were supplied with cattle, grain and bananas. Stanley says:—"An expedition, such as I led, of 800 souls, would, under ordinary circumstances, have needed forty bales of cloth and twenty sacks of beads, as currency to purchase food. Not a bead, or yard of cloth was demanded from us. Such small gifts of cloth as we gave to the chiefs, were given of our own accord."

On August 28, the expedition arrived at Mslala, the Missionary Society's station at the south end of the Victoria Nyanza Lake, under the charge of Mr. Mackay, whom Stanley calls "the modern Livingstone." About a degree west of Mackay's mission station, they discovered the south-western extremity of Lake Victoria. "Our journey," says Stanley, "had led us along an entirely undiscovered portion of the western coast, which was extended to 2° 48′ S. Lat., whence we turned directly east for Usambiro, situated at the termination of the long bay on the south coast of the lake. This considerable extension of the Victoria increases its superficial area, and gives it a length of 270 statute miles."

At the missionary station, Emin Pasha addressed to the Relief Committee, in London, a letter of thanks, in which he says:—"It would be impossible to tell you what has happened here after Mr. Stanley's first start; his graphic pen will tell you everything much better than I could. I hope, also, the Egyptian Government permitting it, some future day to be allowed to present myself before you, and to express to you then the feelings of gratitude my pen would be short in expressing, in a personal interview. Until such happy moments come, I beg to ask you to transmit to all subscribers of the fund, the sincerest thanks of a handful of forlorn people, who through your instrumentality have been saved from destruction and now hope to embrace their relatives. To speak here of Mr. Stanley's and his officers' merits would be inadequate. If I live to return I shall make my acknowledgments."

On their arrival at the missionary station of Mslala, the expedition had traversed, since leaving the Albert Edward Nyanza, "400 miles of an absolutely new region, untraveled and unvisited by any white man," and for three-fourths of this journey they were the recipients of welcome and daily bounties such as are unparalleled in African travel. Once a week Stanley was able, by means of the herds captured from the hostile Wanyoro, and the gifts of the people, to distribute 8000 pounds of meat rations to the entire column.

After a stay of 19 days at the station, the expedition, guided by one of Mr. Mackay's people, resumed its march towards the coast; but they were not destined to complete the journey without serious opposition from the natives. The Wasukuma had been accustomed to stop caravans and extort what they wished. They tried the same course of insolent extortion, and when this was repelled, disputed the advance of the column through their territory for five days. They attacked in great numbers, and, says Stanley, "frequently advanced by hundreds on either flank of the column, but the breachloaders restrained them from reaching the line of march."

On leaving this hostile country they entered friendly territory and thence to Mpwapwa, their progress was unimpeded and without incident. Many European nationalities were now represented in his camp. Besides German, French, Italian, Greek and Egyptians, for whom they acted as escorts, almost every district between Usukuma and Mpwapwa sent new accessions of Africans who were unable to reach the coast or feared oppression by the way, until the column numbered about 1000 souls.

Long before reaching Mpwapwa, however, rumor was busy with the events of the coast. They heard of missionaries murdered and mission-houses burnt, of German officers killed, and coast towns levelled to the ground in retaliation; and at Mpwapwa they witnessed the results of the war in the ruined English mission-house, and the dismantled fort of the German East African Company.

Near Simbaruwemi the expedition received a welcome supply of European comforts, which had been sent by the thoughtful kindness of Major Wissmann, the German Commissioner, and thence each day their hearts were gladdened with kindly notes and gifts from English friends at Zanzibar. At the Kingani Ferry they had the pleasure of meeting Major Wissmann, and being escorted thence to Bagamoyo, and within ten minutes of their arrival the officers were

LANDING OF EMIN PASHA AT KATALI.

seated before a breakfast as sumptuous as any Berlin restaurant could have furnished.*

Out of the number of 570 refugees from the Equatorial Province who had sought convoy to the coast, according to the muster-roll at Kavalli, on April 5, there arrived, on December 4, 1889; at Bagamoyo, on the mainland opposite Zanzibar, only 291 souls. The loss was, therefore, 279, or nearly one-half, during a journey of 1400 miles, but the greater portion of these, about 200, were left under the care of various friendly native chiefs. The remainder, about 80 souls, perished of ulcers, fevers or debility.

"Here," says Stanley, "my duty ended. The Pasha was among his friends. Casati was with the Italian consul, the English officers were with their countrymen, the faithful Zanzibars were in their own land, and I was once more free."

The loss among the members of the expedition was very heavy. Of the 13 Soomaulis, engaged by Major Barttelot at Aden, only one survived the journey. Three of them were killed by natives while foraging for food; nine died from fever and debility. Of the 60 Soudanese enlisted at Cairo, only 12 returned to the coast, seven having been already sent home from Yambuya. Of the 41 thus lost, two suffered the death

---

* After passing unscathed through the dangers of his long residence in Central Africa, surrounded latterly by traitors, Emin Pasha narrowly fell a victim to an accident such as might happen to any stay-at-home old lady anywhere. As Bruce was killed by falling down the stairs of his house in Scotland, after his wanderings in Abyssinia, so Emin Pasha, after the banquet at Bagamoyo in honor of himself and Stanley, walked out of an open window, which, with his impaired sight, he mistook for a door. For many weeks he lingered between life and death, and recovered as by a miracle, thanks chiefly to the care of Surgeon Parke.

penalty for mutiny and murder, and one deserted. Of the 620 Zanzibaris,* only 225 returned to their native island; 55 were killed in the skirmishes which took place between Yambuya and the Albert Nyanza; two were executed for selling their rifles and ammunition to the enemy; 202 died of starvation and disease, and the rest deserted.

Of the Europeans, Major Barttelot was murdered, Mr. Jameson died of fever, and Messrs. Stairs, Nelson, Jephson, Parke, Bonny, Ward and Troup, and Hoffman (Stanley's servant) emerged out of Africa in safety."

Stanley drew special attention to the good service rendered by Lieutenant Stairs, Captain Nelson, Mr. Jephson, and Surgeon Parke, his companions throughout the period embraced between March, 1887, when the expedition started on the land journey on the Lower Congo, and on December 4, 1889, on which date, after crossing the continent of Africa, it reached the port of Bagamoyo on the Indian Ocean. He says:—"Words fail to express my deep feelings of thankfulness that it was my fortune to be blessed with such noble companionship. Never, while human nature remains as we know it, will there be found four gentlemen so matchless for their constancy, devotion to their work, earnest purpose, and unflinching obedience to honor and duty."

* Lieutenant Stairs, second in command of the expedition, said of these faithful Zanzibaris:—"From first to last the Zanzibaris taken round to the Congo behaved in a manner in every way worthy of the situation. They had many difficulties to contend with, but in six months they got to understand the character of the Zanzibaris, and he thought the Zanzibaris understood them, and it was through kindness and firmness they succeeded so well. They treated them as if they were white men and soldiers, and they never failed them. In the open country through which they went they always responded to the whistle of Mr. Stanley, which was sounded in the morning for the march."

Besides effecting their object, the expedition explored about 1200 miles of an unknown region, and made several interesting discoveries. Stanley proved that east and north and north-east of the Congo there exists an immense area of about 250,000 square miles, which is covered by one unbroken forest. He added to our knowledge of the sources of the Nile, to ascertain which so many brave and valuable lives have been sacrificed. Stanley's discovery of the source of the south-west branch of the White Nile is of great interest. He says:—" We now know that the White Nile is formed by the surplus waters of the two lakes, the Victoria and the Albert Edward respectively, to the south-east and south-west, which are received by the Albert, and discharged northward towards the Mediterranean in one grand river, called the Bahr-el-Abiad, or the White River. We also know now the exact limits of the Albert, Victoria, and Albert Edward Lakes, which are embraced within the Nile basin, and are situated near the sources of the famous river. We have discovered the mountains, called by the early Arab geographers, the Mountains of the Moon, and whose snowy tops, known by the modern name, Ruwenzori, furnish the waters which form the Semliki River and the Albert Edward Lake."

The distance traveled in the interior of Africa by Stanley, personally, is estimated by him at 5400 miles, of which all but 1000 miles were on foot. The expedition occupied three years, and rescued nearly 300 persons at a cost of less than $150,000, so that on the lower grounds of economy, its success must be regarded as remarkable.

As we have followed him in all his travels, we will

THE YELLALA FALLS, LOWER CONGO.

give a recapitulation of his discoveries. In company with Livingstone, he explored the northern portion of Lake Tanganyika, and settled, in the negative, the question, then much debated among geographers, whether the Nile did or did not take its rise among those ample waters. Then, upon the second expedition, he traced down the Shimeyu River, which flows from the south, about 300 miles, into the Victoria Nyanza, and is accordingly one of the ultimate sources of the Nile. He circumnavigated the Victoria Nyanza, and discovered Lake Albert Edward. He also circumnavigated Lake Tanganyika, and showed that it discharged its waters into the Lualaba through the Opoco. Then he traced the Lualaba itself, which he proved to be the Congo, thus settling the question which had perplexed the mind of Livingstone so much in his last years. Lastly, he traced the Congo down to the sea, "through an Odyssey of wandering and an Iliad of combat," and by that means, he threw open to the enterprise of Europe a territory fully as large as British India. Throughout all his journeys, Stanley was his own surveyor, his own astronomical observer, and the recorder of his own actions. Like Ulysses, he had seen many races, and had traversed many lands; and he has said that his journeys in Abyssinia and Ashantee, in search of Livingstone, across Africa, the expeditions up the Congo, and the last, to relieve Emin Pasha, covered about 24,000 miles of ground.

Honors and congratulations were showered from many lands upon Stanley for his last great journey, perhaps the most remarkable in the whole history of travel: in Egypt, by the Khedive and all the nationalities who congregate in the winter at Cairo, that cosmopolitan resort; in Belgium, by its enlightened ruler, and all classes among his subjects; and in England, which is proud to claim the Welshman as one of her own sons. The English people appreciated the magnitude of the discoveries made by Stanley; the brilliance of his last achievement, and the remarkable combination of qualities which have made him pre-eminent among modern explorers.

The statements of Stanley's cruelty and disregard for human life are baseless. He was most forbearing throughout his last journey; and only attacked the natives when they refused to permit the expedition to proceed on its march and attacked him. Then he brushed them on one side, but with no needless slaughter. As to the stories of his executing many of his followers, he only inflicted the death penalty on four.*

He risked his life, and a reputation as an explorer who had never known failure; success, therefore, could add little to his fame, whereas he imperilled everything an ambitious man, or self-seeker, values.

Stanley's training as a soldier in the Confederate army was serviceable when promptitude and decision were required in dealing with the traitors under Emin Pasha's

---

* He writes on this head: " I had to execute four men during our expedition: two for stealing rifles, cartridges and ammunition; one of the Pasha's people for conspiracy, theft and decoying about thirty women belonging to the Egyptians, besides for seditious plots—court-martialed by all officers and sentenced to be hung; a Soudanese soldier, the last, who deliberately proceeded to a friendly tribe and began shooting at the natives. One man was shot dead instantly and another was seriously wounded. The chief came and demanded justice, the people were mustered, the murderer and his companions were identified, the identification by his companions confirmed, and the murderer was delivered to them according to the law of 'blood for blood.' "

command, and his readiness as a sailor who had served in the Federal navy was equally valuable in enabling him to deal with any unexpected difficulty in the line of march.

Throughout the expedition Stanley displayed a high courage and cheerful spirit that no evil fortune could daunt, and a fertility of resource that was equal to any demand made upon it. Where he was present success smiled upon the expedition, but in his absence failure ensued, only to disappear with his advent on the scene. These qualities, the success he attained when confronted with well-nigh insurmountable difficulties, the immense extent of ground covered during his travels, amounting as he has said, to some 24,000 miles, and the magnitude and importance of his discoveries, fully entitle him to take rank as the " Napoleon of African Travel."

www.ingramcontent.com/pod-product-compliance
Lightning Source LLC
Chambersburg PA
CBHW021346230426
43666CB00006B/426